BIG BANG DISRUPTION

'A stimulating read . . . carefully researched and accessibly written . . . the case studies on disruption alone are worth the cover price' *Financial Times*

'Downes and Nunes are right that the competitive heat has been turned up by new technology' *Economist*

'*Big Bang Disruption* elegantly and simply identifies why innovation happens in some new companies and how you can embrace and harness this new way of thinking' Dick Costolo, CEO, Twitter

'People think in straight lines and are surprised when there is a sharp take-off. Larry Downes and Paul Nunes teach us to anticipate exponential growth and think outside the line and on to the curve. Their observations on life and business are seminal for the way we work and live' Andy Lippman, associate director, MIT Media Lab

'As *Jaws* was to summer blockbusters, *Big Bang Disruption* is to business cycles; it presents a playbook for new opportunities and new dangers. It's also as scary as *Jaws* but it's better to know what everyone else will soon see than to bury one's head in the sand and pretend these disruptors don't exist' Blair Levin, communications and society fellow, Aspen Institute

'Big bangs are everywhere and are happening faster each year and with bigger impact. People in every industry would be well advised to follow the unconventional strategies outlined in this book. *Big Bang Disruption* got my company energized to innovate ahead of the curve and drive change rather than become victims' Kandy Anand, President and CEO, Molson Coors International

'Wow! *Big Bang Disruption* beautifully captures how technology has changed the speed and cycle of innovation. It is a primer on dizzying change in many industries and a strategy manual for any entrepreneur or CEO who must understand disruptive innovation to survive and prosper. A compelling must-read' Gary Shapiro, President and CEO, Consumer Electronics Association

ABOUT THE AUTHORS

Larry Downes is an internet industry analyst and author on the impact of disruptive technologies on business and policy. His first book, *Unleashing the Killer App*, was one of the biggest business bestsellers of the early 2000s. He is a columnist for Forbes and CNET and writes regularly for other publications including *USA Today* and the *Harvard Business Review*. He lives in Berkeley, California.

Paul Nunes is the Global Managing Director of Research at the Accenture Institute for High Performance and the senior contributing editor at *Outlook*, Accenture's journal of thought leadership. His most recent book is *Jumping the S-Curve*. His research findings have been covered by *The New York Times*, the *Wall Street Journal*, *USA Today* and Forbes. He lives in Boston.

BIG BANG DISRUPTION

BUSINESS SURVIVAL IN THE AGE OF CONSTANT INNOVATION

LARRY DOWNES
AND PAUL NUNES

PORTFOLIO
PENGUIN

PORTFOLIO PENGUIN

UK | USA | Canada | Ireland | Australia
India | New Zealand | South Africa

Portfolio Penguin is part of the Penguin Random House group of companies
whose addresses can be found at global.penguinrandomhouse.com.

First published in the United States of America by Portfolio/Penguin,
a member of Penguin Group (USA) Inc. 2014
First published in Great Britain by Portfolio Penguin 2014
This edition published 2015
001

Printed in Great Britain by Clays Ltd, St Ives plc

A CIP catalogue record for this book is available from the British Library

ISBN: 978–0–241–00353–4

www.greenpenguin.co.uk

CONTENTS

CONTENTS

BIG BANG DISRUPTION

INTRODUCTION

Address books, video cameras, pagers, wristwatches, maps, books, travel games, flashlights, home telephones, dictation recorders, cash registers, Walkmen, Day-Timers, alarm clocks, answering machines, yellow pages, wallets, keys, phrase books, transistor radios, personal digital assistants, dashboard navigation systems, remote controls, airline ticket counters, newspapers and magazines, directory assistance, travel and insurance agents, restaurant guides and pocket calculators.

What do these things all have in common?

Each has, or is in the process of becoming, a victim of Big Bang Disruption, a new kind of innovation with the power to undermine stable businesses in a matter of months or even days.

The speed and the dramatic impact of Big Bang Disruption are the result of disruptive technologies that continue to enter the market better and cheaper than their predecessors. In this brave new world, new products and services start out life competing simultaneously on price, performance, and customization.

Thanks to ubiquitous high-speed (or "broadband") computing networks, standards, and the rapid deployment of over a billion mobile devices, consumers around the world can discover these breakthroughs—the Big Bang Disruptors—as soon as they come into existence. Marketing is led not from above, but by the users themselves, who drive much of the buzz (and customer service) through social networks, review sites, microblogging platforms, and other information-sharing tools.

The often counterintuitive behavior of these new disruptors and the innovators who create them has already redefined the rules of engagement in highly competitive, technology intensive industries, including consumer electronics, computing, and communications. But as the computing revolution continues to insinuate itself into every corner of our lives, Big Bang Disruptors are starting to appear in every industry.

For each of the items listed above, for example, the source of disruption is the same—the programmable smartphone, a hybrid computing and communications device with an endless number of small software apps. Apps can be small because most of their data processing takes place elsewhere, in what is known as cloud computing. This combination of hardware, software, and distributed computing have quickly replaced a wide range of devices, products, and services; some very old and others relatively recent innovations themselves.

Well beyond individual products and services, the very process of innovation is being disrupted. The companies and entrepreneurs that build Big Bang Disruptors don't practice business as usual. Instead of developing their products in secret, they work in the open, letting early users test and extend each iteration of their design. Rather than relying on proprietary technologies and research methods, they simply combine increasingly cheap off-the-shelf hardware and software components, and then release the result into the market.

If they fail, they fail quickly. If they succeed, the early users become collaborators and even investors, jump-starting the leap to mainstream markets.

Once the disruptors arrive, there's little chance for a competitive response. The supply chains of mature industries offering goods that are suddenly yesterday's inferior alternatives are suddenly destabilized, even devastated. If you haven't learned to see the disruptors coming long before your customers do, it's game over.

For incumbents and their carefully constructed strategic plans, Big Bang Disruption is the innovator's disaster.

This book will help you avoid that disaster.

But first, an introduction. Separately and together, we have been studying the evolution of disruptive innovations most of our careers. *Big Bang Disruption* builds on our previous books, including *Unleashing the Killer App* and *Jumping the S-Curve*, which looked at the impact of new technologies on the strategies and processes that drive modern enterprises.

Killer App was an early look at how the Internet and other digital technologies moved from back office to front, driving strategic change rather than simply supporting it.

Jumping the S-Curve similarly explored the ever-shrinking gap in time between one wave of disruptive technologies and the next. It offered crucial advice for business leaders determined to survive the increasingly traumatic transitions between them.

The heart of *Big Bang Disruption*, however, is our continuing multiyear study of the changing nature of disruptive innovation, analysis we are conducting in conjunction with the Accenture Institute for High Performance. This research looks at the nature of competition and strategic change in over thirty different industry segments, with over a hundred detailed case studies—many recent but some historical.

We have cataloged dozens of Big Bang Disruptors that have appeared seemingly without warning to devastate the plans of some of the best-known companies in the world, sometimes fatally. And we have conducted in-depth interviews with entrepreneurs, investors, and executives in businesses old and new. We have learned their secrets for spotting potential disruptors sooner than their competitors, and for finding the fastest and least expensive ways of experimenting with them to determine whether, or when, they are ready for prime time.

Many of the most dramatic examples, not surprisingly, come from some of the most admired technology innovators of the new century—including companies such as Google, Apple, Samsung, Sony, and Microsoft. Others will come from enterprises you may not have heard of until recently, if at all, including start-ups such as Airbnb, Uber, Kickstarter, and Udacity.

Still others come from incumbent companies that have learned the techniques of Big Bang Disruption, delivering dramatic new products and services that leverage their existing assets and abilities. Some aren't even companies at all—just experiments that turned into dramatic success stories without necessarily intending to. In the pages that follow, you will meet academics, artists, and even one high school student who have managed, if only by accident, to create Big Bang Disruptors whose arrival unsettled the strategies of large public companies.

We did not, of course, begin our work with a clean slate. There is already a vast and growing literature on the impact of disruptive technologies on the formation and execution of business strategy, including books to which we have contributed. While there's little point to reviewing this work in detail, much of what has been written, particularly the work of Joseph Schumpeter, Peter Drucker, and historian Thomas Kuhn, remains not only valid but essential reading. (Researcher Carlota Perez, we should also note, made slightly different use of the term "big bang" to denote revolutionary technologies—the kind that attracted killer apps.)

But our findings on the process of Big Bang Disruption have also opened a wide rift with older views of strategy and competition. We want to describe briefly the source of that break.

Over the course of the last twenty-five years, academic thinking on disruptive innovation has evolved through three distinct eras.

Before the information age, conventional wisdom held that new markets were created from the top down. Innovators create differentiated goods targeted to customers who could afford to pay more and were willing to do so. Often earning the title of "luxury goods," thanks to learned efficiency and economies of scale these goods would later trickle down to mass markets in the form of similar if scaled-down versions sold at lower prices.

Think of all the one-time options on automobiles that were once considered luxuries but which now come standard on most cars—power steering, locks, windows and brakes, high-end sound systems, even sunroofs. Yet the real cost of an entry-level luxury car today is well below the price for an average vehicle in the 1950s.

According to Harvard Business School professor Michael Porter, companies can achieve competitive advantage only by innovating along one of three "generic" strategies, each of which implements the top-down approach in a different way. Companies are urged either to differentiate their market offerings with special features that justify a premium price, or to optimize production efficiencies and sell at a lower price than competitors. Porter's third generic strategy is a variation on the first two, focused on serving just one segment of the market extremely well. Low cost and high value, however, just don't mix.

But in his important 1997 book *The Innovator's Dilemma*, Clayton Christensen challenged the top-down view of innovation, and argued persuasively that disruptors often work from the bottom up. In this, the second era of disruptive innovation theory, disruptive technologies start life less valuable and feature rich than those the current market supports, but at a significantly better price—at least for customers who will accept lower quality.

In one famous example, Christensen demonstrated how excavation equipment based on new hydraulic actuators ultimately displaced older cable-driven machinery. Early hydraulic diggers were cheaper, but were too weak to handle big jobs. So their makers created a niche market by selling small backhoes that could excavate the basements of suburban homes.

That was a market that was too small for producers of heavy-duty shovels to care about. But over time, as hydraulic technology improved, the abilities of the smaller machines improved to compete for the business of every customer segment of the incumbents. Eventually, hydraulics could do everything the cable machines could do, and at a better price. The disrupters displaced many of the older companies, and became the industry's new leaders.

To avoid the "innovator's dilemma," Christensen urges incumbents to watch for disruptive technologies in the form of lower-quality substitutes that enter the market first by picking off the least-profitable customers and then, as the technology improves, moving up to become competitive with market leaders. In this model, executives who see the early signs of disruption are believed to have plenty of time to respond by testing the new technology and preparing to shift when price and performance make it acceptable to mainstream customers.

In the third stage of strategic thinking on innovation, W. Chan Kim and Renée Mauborgne, the authors of *Blue Ocean Strategy*, update the bottom-up view of gradual disruption with examples of innovators who stop thinking about traditional products and traditional competitors altogether. Rather, these disrupters tap into new and unmet needs in existing, even mature, categories—coming at them more or less sideways.

By understanding the range of values customers place on different product and service feature combinations, according to this view, innovators can offer more of some and less of others, targeted at a particular segment of the market. Cirque du Soleil, the authors explain, adopted many of the features of a traditional circus, but lowered costs by cutting out star performers, animal shows, and multiple show arenas. It then added features such as artistic choreography and unique venues. Cirque du Soleil created a "blue ocean," commanding far higher prices than the average circus, enjoyed by a group of customers who might not otherwise be interested in circus acts at all.

We have entered a fourth stage of innovation—the era of Big Bang Disruption. The new disrupters attack existing markets not just from the top, bottom, and sides, but from all three at once. By tying their products to the exponential growth and falling costs of new technologies, their offerings can be simultaneously better, cheaper, and more customized. Not just for one group of users, but for all (or nearly all) customers. This isn't disruptive innovation. It's devastating innovation.

The suddenness with which Big Bang Disruption can occur presents an insurmountable obstacle for traditional academic approaches to strategy. The meticulously prepared strategic plans of Porter can be neutralized in an instant. The relatively leisurely pace of response recommended by Christensen, and even the clever search for blue oceans no one else has yet navigated, can each be catastrophic. Expecting markets will stand still while you innovate selectively to improve quality or price is a very dangerous assumption.

Your new competition operates without any of your constraints and doesn't play by the old rules. Their Big Bang Disruptors may not even be intended to compete with your products. You may simply be collateral damage in their frenetic efforts to find new markets and to capture the attention of as many customers as quickly as they can.

This book is divided into two roughly equal parts. We begin by exploring the strange anatomy of Big Bang Disruption—its origins, its execution, and its often dramatic impact. We then show you what you need to know to survive its arrival in your industry, and what you can do to harness its remarkable potential to remake your business and redefine your markets.

Though we primarily address executives in existing businesses, the lessons of Big Bang Disruption apply equally to entrepreneurs starting their first enterprise—who, if successful, will become incumbents soon enough. Regardless of your job title, industry, or the size of your organization's balance sheet, your new priority must be to create, launch, and compete against these new disruptors. For that reason, we refer to the practitioners of Big Bang Disruption, whether working in start-ups or incumbent businesses, as innovators.

Part I dissects the phenomenon of Big Bang Disruption—what it looks like (Chapter One), the economics that drive it (Chapter Two), and the unusual life cycle of its rises and falls (Chapter Three).

Part II will show you how to reinvent your organization to create your own Big Bang Disruptors, and to avoid fatal collisions with those launched by others in your direction. This section is organized around the four distinct stages of the Big Bang life cycle, which we have named after analogous periods in the like-named theory that describes the creation and eventual end of the known universe: The Singularity (Chapter Four), The Big Bang (Chapter Five), The Big Crunch (Chapter Six), and Entropy (Chapter Seven). Figure 1 shows the ominously shaped figure that illustrates the four stages, a figure that, for obvious reasons, we have nicknamed the shark fin.

Part I is the diagnosis of Big Bang Disruption. Part II is the treatment. Where most business books only provide one of these services (usually the first), in the spirit of better and cheaper innovation, we have attempted to deliver both.

Part II is organized around twelve new rules for Big Bang Disruption—the best practices of companies across industries that have used this new approach to innovation to disrupt markets. Together, the rules comprise a Big Bang Disruption model for strategy and execution, essential to launching not just one disruptor but to recreating your enterprise as an engine of continuing innovation. Each is introduced through detailed examples of enterprises of all

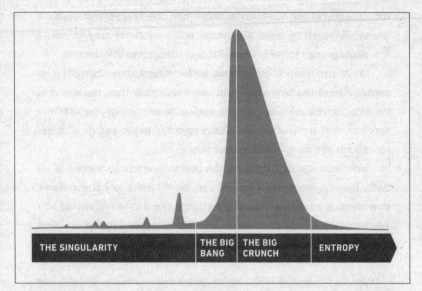

FIGURE 1. The Shark Fin

shapes and sizes that have used these rules to create or survive Big Bang Disruption in each of its four phases.

On the subject of examples, we want to pause for a moment to make a confident prediction. If you're reading this book even a few years after its publication, many of the products and services we will describe as Big Bang Disruptors, and the companies that launched them, will have disappeared, or at the very least fallen off their perches as leading innovators.

Each of the examples we use—positive and negative—were chosen because of the insights they offer on particular aspects of the Big Bang Disruption process, and of success or failure at each stage. We don't expect many of today's disruptors to continue delivering unprecedented value for their creators, at least not in the forms we last saw them.

Big Bang Disruptors, as we will explain, often have very short lives. As hard as they are to create and introduce at just the right time, the real magic is in creating more than one. Few enterprises have mastered the art of serial disruption, and even those may be only a few management missteps away from an unrecoverable decline.

We're also unapologetic about the fact that many—though by no means all—of the case studies in this book come from the world of consumer electronics, computing, and communications products and services, with a particular emphasis on cloud-based mobile technologies such as smartphones and tablets.

Mobile computing is one of the fastest growing industries of all time. During the worst years of the most recent global economic downturn, it was often the only one that seemed to be registering any kind of growth and optimism among consumers and producers. And there are other reasons for focusing on the mobile industry:

- *Speed*—The quick replacement cycle for new products and services in mobile computing—devices and apps alike—make it the most visible industry where Big Bang Disruption is happening today. It is the easiest place to see what works and what doesn't as innovators work out the new rules of strategy, competition, product development, sourcing, marketing, and customer service. Each new generation of devices is accompanied by new business innovations, offering valuable lessons for executives in any business who study them carefully.

- *Platform*—Mobile computing is the jumping-off point for the disruption of any industry where timely access to relevant information can alter consumer behavior—which is to say, any industry. If an app hasn't disrupted at least part of your business today, it soon will. So even companies far from the center of the storm need to understand how mobile technology is evolving, and the many directions in which the ripples of its disruptions are spreading.

- *Scale*—With over a billion smartphones and tablets already in the hands of eager consumers, entrepreneurs have easy access to once-expensive custom-made parts, including displays, sensors, processors, and reusable software. Everything from fitness monitoring devices to personal drone aircraft are being manufactured using off-the-shelf component parts originally designed for mobile computing.
- *Ecosystem*—The mobile industry has also become the most advanced example of an industry that exhibits a key feature of Big Bang Disruption—the replacement of a traditional supply chain with an ecosystem. Instead of the largely static, one-way flow of information and goods from raw materials to consumers, ecosystems emphasize intense interaction in multiple directions, competitive discipline exerted on every participant by all of the others, and an ability to quickly form new partnerships, ventures, and enterprises as technologies evolve.

The book also features a disproportionate number of examples from companies in the United States and East Asia, a bias for which we are slightly more apologetic. Today, thanks in large part to a tradition of entrepreneurial research universities, favorable tax treatment for investments in start-ups, and laws that promote the free flow of information and of entrepreneurial talent, the United States has the clear lead in developing Big Bang Disruptors. Tomorrow, depending on how governments themselves react to the growing challenges of disruptive technologies, that lead may shrink or even disappear.

The twelve rules of Big Bang Disruption, in any case, know no national borders. Technology hubs are opening pretty much anywhere there is the high-speed Internet access necessary for rapid development and instant access to suppliers and customers. From Kansas City to Moscow, from London to Nairobi, and from Santiago to

Davao in the Philippines, a new generation of entrepreneurs is quickly learning the ways of hackathons, crowdfunding, and combinatorial innovation we describe in the pages that follow.

We fully expect that our future research will take us far from Silicon Valley, and we look forward to seeing how other cultures leave their own mark on the processes and best practices described in this book.

The spread of Big Bang Disruption around the world underscores our belief that, while daunting, almost any enterprise can reinvent itself to meet these new competitive pressures. But the time to begin is now. As the pace of technological change continues to accelerate, integrating these rules into the day-to-day activities of every member of your executive team, and of every employee and business partner, provides the best hope we can offer of finding yourself featured as the next example of an enterprise that has created phenomenal new value by disrupting its markets.

How well we have succeeded is up to you to decide. Let us know, using whatever information sharing technology you prefer. We genuinely want to hear from you—about the model, about the process, and about examples of success and failure that you come across. Using Facebook, Twitter, and our "Big Bang Disruption" column on Forbes.com, we have done our best to crowdsource the book, collecting as much material from our readers as from our own research.

Like the enterprises we study, we expect to change our practices dramatically in the next cycle and in those that come afterward. Follow us, join us, take us to task. As our research has made clear, that's the best source of new ideas for innovators dedicated to making things better.

Larry Downes, Berkeley, CA
Paul Nunes, Boston, MA
October 2013

PART 1
BIG BANG
DISRUPTION

CHAPTER 1
WHAT IS BIG BANG DISRUPTION?
COMPETING IN A WORLD OF BETTER AND CHEAPER

For most of the twentieth century, the production and distribution of road maps was a mature industry dominated by a few leading companies including Rand McNally, Thomas Guides, and not-for-profit automobile clubs.

But with the growth of home computing and the Internet, a new kind of competition arrived. Initial threats came in the form of free Internet-based maps and driving directions from sites including MapQuest and Yahoo, which used digitized map data to offer users the ability to zoom in and out, and later, to overlay satellite photos and highlight selected features, such as the location of restaurants and gas stations.

Then came stand-alone and in-dash devices that utilize high-precision data from satellite-based Global Positioning Systems (GPS) to generate optimal routes and turn-by-turn spoken directions. Companies such as Garmin, TomTom, and Magellan competed fiercely, offering new models that were increasingly more sophisticated and more compact than their predecessors.

With improvements in technology and production economies of scale, GPS devices quickly moved from luxury items to affordable goods. Garmin's first commercial product, for example, sold in 1991 for $2,500. By 2000, the company had sold three million devices, and retail prices for some units fell as low as $120. As the printed map market shrank, Rand McNally acquired its longtime competitor Thomas Guides. Still, consolidation wasn't enough to compete. After more than one hundred years as a family-owned business, Rand McNally fell apart, and was quickly sold off in pieces. By 2003, what had been the commercial mapmaking unit was bankrupt.

The true disruptor, however, turned out to be the smartphone, a device neither designed nor intended to compete with traditional navigation aids. Cloud-based smartphone apps, such as the free and perpetually unfinished Google Maps Navigation, accelerated the reconfiguration of an already fragile industry. Launched in 2009, the product extended Google's existing mapping database and directional software, adding voice directions, GPS integration, real-time traffic, and connections to other apps including search, e-mail, and address books.

Google also included the navigation app as part of the standard release of every new version of its Android operating system, making it available to any of the millions of users who might want to give it a try. As with most of the company's software products, Google Maps Navigation was offered for free—or rather, in exchange for permission to present more advertising to users.

Free is easy when manufacturing and distribution costs are low, and when you can rely, as many software-based services do, on reusable information and indirect sources of revenue. For Google Maps Navigation, development costs have been relatively modest. Much of the software and the data it uses already existed, created at significant expense by Google over the previous decade.

The rest came from public sources, notably from satellites designed and operated for intelligence purposes by the U.S. Department of

Defense. That data had existed for decades, but only became available for private use in 1996, when President Bill Clinton ordered it declassified.

"Obviously we like the price of free, because consumers like that as well," Google CEO Eric Schmidt said at the time.

For users, the navigation app adds virtually nothing to the cost of ownership or maintenance of the device; for Google, per-user costs are trivial. Consumers already pay for the device and the network, and the app takes up a minimal amount of storage and uses little of the data connection. The map data is stored and most of the processing takes place remotely on Google's servers. Updates to the software are automatically installed on the user's phone. Google Maps Navigation's developers don't do any marketing or sales.

With the growing popularity of the Android operating system, success of the Google product was pretty much guaranteed. Within a year, the navigation app had one hundred million users, a number that doubled less than a year later. When a new version was released for Apple devices in 2012, users downloaded it over ten million times in the first forty-eight hours. It's hard even to estimate how many users have the product now.

App-based services operate, needless to say, under a very different model than traditional businesses. Before the apps showed up, Garmin, TomTom, and Magellan had developed a robust business making and selling stand-alone electronic navigators that performed the same functions. At the time Google released its navigation app into the cloud, traditional navigation devices were still selling—and selling well—for hundreds of dollars.

Google claims it wasn't looking to disrupt the business of these companies. Yet from the outset, the app outperformed the stand-alone navigation devices on every competitive dimension. Being free was clearly cheaper.

And Google architected its offering to be better by keeping most of the mapping data and route calculation in the cloud, making it easy to continually update and enhance the product. Unlike most stand-alone GPS devices, Google's app doesn't store maps on the device. So they don't become outdated or require time-consuming and often expensive updates.

By connecting with other smartphone services, the free product also offers a more integrated solution. (Search the Web for a nearby restaurant and hit the navigation button to go right to directions.) And it does so for nearly every customer segment, from consumers to enterprise users.

Google continues to improve its product. In 2013, the company paid a reported $1 billion to buy Israeli software company Waze, which relies on user-submitted data to create and improve its maps and navigation, and provides easy-to-use tools for users to report errors, shortcuts, and traffic conditions. Waze, launched in 2008, had fifty million users at the time of the acquisition. Google is integrating the new technology into its navigation product, enhancements for which its users will continue to pay nothing.

While the incumbent GPS device makers still offer specialized in-dashboard units and proprietary apps that vie with free alternatives from Google and others, it's hard to compete with better and cheaper. The day Google announced Google Maps Navigation, the share price of traditional navigation device makers fell more than 15 percent, a drop that accelerated a decline that began with the release of Apple's iPhone.

Between 2008 and 2012, TomTom's consumer revenue fell by more than half; Garmin's automotive and mobile sales fell 40 percent. Eighteen months after the introduction of Google Maps Navigation, the makers of stand-alone GPS devices had lost as much as 85 percent of their market value.

BETTER AND CHEAPER

Mobile navigation apps are an example of what we call a Big Bang Disruptor, an innovation that, from the moment of its creation, is both better and cheaper than the products and services against which it competes. Using new technologies including the Internet, cloud-based computing, and increasingly powerful and ubiquitous computing devices, Big Bang Disruptors can destabilize mature industries in record time, leaving incumbents and their supply-chain partners dazed, and, soon after, devastated.

Drive down any downtown street and look at the empty storefronts. Many of them were recently occupied by bookstores, camera retailers and film processors, office supply shops, post offices, travel agencies, and big-box electronics and appliance sellers—all victims of the ongoing revolution in increasingly powerful mobile computing devices. The mobile revolution may prove as profoundly transformational as the first wave of computing itself.

Yet there was little reason to imagine when smartphones were introduced in the late 1990s that they were anything more than a modest upgrade to notoriously unreliable cellular telephones. They were expensive, with limited capacity for data and video. There were few, if any, third-party applications. The networks they used were slow and often unpredictable.

But with the launch of Apple's iPhone in 2007 and, soon after, Google's open-source Android operating system, smartphones have transformed into full-fledged mobile computers—engines for the expedited creation and delivery of Big Bang Disruptors. There are more than a billion smartphone customers worldwide.

Today's models come standard with high-definition displays and cameras, ample memory, data storage, and extended batteries. Over the last decade, mobile network operators have invested hundreds of billions of dollars to create next-generation 4G LTE and WiFi broadband coverage worldwide.

That investment has been driven by another critical feature of the smartphone ecosystem: cloud-based computing. Because the device maintains a high-speed connection to the network, data storage and data processing on the smartphone can be kept to a minimum. Most of it happens on infrastructure operated by service providers, including network operators, content companies, and other third parties.

For app developers, that architecture dramatically accelerates the speed of product development even as it reduces risk. To design and launch an app, you don't need to invest in a substantial computing and communications infrastructure. If the app is successful, you can easily scale your IT resources up and down to support changing customer needs, renting servers and even application software in a highly competitive virtual market. Updates and even new versions can be deployed frequently, without inconveniencing users.

Little surprise, then, that today there are thousands of app developers, some of whom have become multibillion-dollar companies in record time. By 2013, according to the trade group Mobile Future, consumers were downloading one hundred million apps. Every day.

In the last few years, says 451 Research's Peter Christy, cloud computing has reversed the IT advantage long held by large enterprises over small businesses. "We've reached the moment when you get all the benefits of IT without any obligations for competence or infrastructure," he said. Start-ups can make immediate use of the best and cheapest cloud services without the need for internal IT, or to integrate or customize incompatible software.

Large enterprises, on the other hand, are moving more slowly to the cloud, held back, Christy says, by "twenty years of legacy IT investment decisions that first need to be erased."

But the phenomenon of Big Bang Disruption, as we'll see, isn't just about the mobile ecosystem, nor is its impact limited to the computer and consumer electronics industries. Thanks to dramatic changes in the core economics of innovation in general, every industry is now at risk from competitors that enter the market simultaneously better and cheaper.

Indeed, nearly everything you know about strategy and innovation has suddenly become wrong. Big Bang Disruptors don't follow the traditional rules of competition. They don't target high-end customer segments with a premium alternative. They don't strip down a mature, feature-rich offering for value-conscious customers. They don't deconstruct existing products and pitch them to a new market.

The disrupters don't even see you as competition. They don't share your approach to customer service. They're not sizing up your product line to offer slightly better price or performance with hopes of gaining a short-term advantage. Usually, they're just tossing something shiny in the direction of your customers, hoping to attract them to a business that's completely different from yours.

Worse, Big Bang Disruptors are arriving faster and dispatching incumbents more quickly than ever. Once they hit the market, there's no time for a strategic response. Where disruptive innovations may have once taken a decade or more to transform the affected industries, our research shows that time frame has compressed to half that time—and continues to shrink.

EXPONENTIAL TECHNOLOGIES

To survive Big Bang Disruption, you'll need early warning systems that can see both broader and more deeply into potential new technologies and their impact than even your best competitive radar does today. You'll also need new ways of working with the disruptors, and partnering with their inventors, long before they release commercial products and services.

But before we look at strategies for creating and responding to them, we need to understand what's causing the transformation.

One obvious driver, as we've already suggested, is the ongoing revolution in information technology. In 1965, Intel cofounder Gordon Moore predicted that the processing power of the semiconductor—the basic building block of computing—would continue to get twice as fast every twelve to twenty-four months even as price held constant, a prediction that came to be known as Moore's Law. Moore thought the improvements would continue for at least five years. But Moore's Law still applies, nearly fifty years later.

In IT, evidence of persistent doublings in improvements of both price and performance is clearly visible beyond raw computing power. Related technologies, including data storage, memory, and data communications, have long experienced similar levels of improvement. Combined with the networking standards of the Internet and the unique properties of software, which can be duplicated and distributed at almost no marginal cost, these advances have created an environment in which innovations can be developed and launched quickly and cheaply, disrupting industries far from the world of computing.

Digital technology is not the only field benefiting from exponential growth. Every day, it seems, we read of some new scientific breakthrough that could, if made practical and scalable, translate into Big Bang Disruptors as potent as those generated by better and cheaper computing power.

These include prototypes of buildings fueled by living colonies of algae, or of three-dimensional printers adapted to produce working human organs, organic display technologies that can be rolled up and put in your pocket, or products made of graphene, a sheet of carbon one atom thick with remarkable qualities in conductivity and material strength that are only just being tested.

Economists—who clearly failed their marketing courses as

students—refer to these spectacular innovations as "general-purpose technologies." We prefer to call them "exponential technologies," a term we define as advances that promise repeated doublings in improvement of both price and performance over relatively short intervals, possibly as often as every year or two. Exponential technologies are the platforms from which innovators launch their Big Bang Disruptors.

As the economic downturn that began in 2007 comes to an end, exponential technology is once again the most important driver of global economic growth. The magic of traditional innovation hubs such as Silicon Valley has spread around the world, from South Korea's Daejeon to Moscow's Skolkovo. In popular media, slang, and even in fashion, entrepreneurs, investors, and engineers have once again become role models. As one Silicon Valley venture capitalist recently told us, "It's truly 'The Revenge of the Nerds.'"

Outside of computing, exponential growth is also visible, though less well established, in fields that include stem cell research, renewable energy, human genomics, fiber optics, LEDs, and robotics. In materials science alone, impressive breakthroughs in water splitting, supercapacitors, photonics, thermoelectrics, and energy storage materials have started a rush of investing and development activity, each with the potential for exponential growth.

There is good cause for the optimism of technology boosters. Rough estimates suggest that the next generation of exponential technologies will generate trillions of dollars of new value in the coming decade. We already have concrete examples outside of computing. In medicine, for example, a complete sequencing of one person's DNA, which cost $3 billion a decade ago, now costs only $1,500.

Throughout this book, we will explore dozens of examples of Big Bang Disruptors built with exponential technologies. For the most part, however, we will focus on digital technologies, and for two very good reasons. One is that of all the exponential technologies, computing power has been doubling the longest, and is now producing enough examples of disruptive innovation to fill several books. While this is not a book about the computing revolution, the accelerated appearance of Big Bang Disruptors in consumer electronics, computing, and communications are often the most visible and the most dramatic.

The second reason is that to some degree, all exponential technologies rely on ubiquitous computing power, cloud services, broadband networks, and the Internet to continue their march toward commercial products and services. According to recent reports, annual IT spending passed $2 trillion for the first time in 2013. The digital revolution is not only the most mature, in other words; it is also enabling technological revolutions in areas far from computing.

Indeed, the IT revolution has run long enough to demonstrate just how remarkable doubling the performance of each succeeding generation of an exponential technology can be. Consider that in the 1950s, when commercial computers were first being sold, they were the exclusive domain of specialized applications that required massive data processing and calculations—the U.S. census, for example, or balancing the books of the world's then-largest corporations, such as General Electric. They were large, expensive, and temperamental—operated only by specially trained engineers and maintained in climate-controlled environments.

Because of their cost and complexity, computers were initially relegated to the back office, processing payroll or accounting or manufacturing scheduling. But with each new generation of better and cheaper processors, computing devices have moved closer and closer to the edge of every business—to the point of direct contact, and perhaps even full collaboration, with customers, suppliers, regulators, and competitors.

Computers don't just become better and cheaper incrementally. Even as the size and energy requirements of computers shrink, their processing capacity continues to double, frequently and predictably. Exponential improvement has driven computing from the realm of science fiction to that of a basic commodity.

That means that whether you are buying or selling consumer goods, energy, health care, education, or financial services, the disruptive potential of digital products and services are aimed squarely at your business. Our research into the causes and effects of Big Bang Disruption makes clear that no industry will be left unscathed, no supply chain left unscrambled, no strategic plan left unraveled.

If they have not already arrived, the Big Bang Disruptors are, at the very least, massing at the borders of your industry. Some businesses will have more time to react, and some much less. But every enterprise will be affected by better and cheaper alternatives to technologies that are core to today's business—and perhaps which have been core since the industry first came into existence.

That's because one way or the other, today every business is a digital business. Even if you deal in large, expensive, long-lived goods such as electric generators, or run a medical practice serving hundreds of individual patients, the nature of computing has already utterly changed how you do business.

Consider the fate of specialized medical lab Sleep HealthCenters. Until recently, patients suffering from sleep disorders, such as apnea, needed expensive overnight visits to sleep clinics, including Sleep HealthCenters, to diagnose their ailments. The company, launched in 1997, expanded quickly, with over two dozen locations and revenue that grew from nearly $10 million in 2004 to $30 million in 2010.

But rapid improvements in the price and performance of wearable monitoring devices changed the business, gradually at first, and then suddenly. The more comfortable home setting, for one thing, produced more effective measurements. And rapid declines in the cost of wearable monitoring meant patients could get the same results at a third the price of an overnight stay at a clinic. By 2011, Sleep HealthCenters's revenue started to decline, and the company closed 20 percent of its locations. In 2012, insurance companies decided to cover the less expensive option. Sleep HealthCenters abruptly shut down.

Even when traditional goods and services aren't being replaced with digital alternatives, information technology is firmly integrated as a tool in basic research, product design, sourcing, manufacturing, logistics, sales, marketing, and service. Every link in the supply chain has been altered, and for the better.

Products can be better designed and more precisely made, customer feedback is instantaneous and direct, and pricing, availability, and performance are increasingly transparent. Automobiles last longer and require less frequent maintenance and repair, as do many other durable goods including large appliances. As one client of ours put it recently, you hardly ever hear people say "They don't make 'em like they used to" anymore.

For an increasingly wide range of goods and services, each new generation of offerings gets noticeably and often dramatically better. To the extent that production costs for new goods rely on cheap computing power and software, prices are also falling.

Due to the impact of persistent inflation, "better" is often easier to see than "cheaper," especially outside of computers and consumer electronics. When inflation is low, as it has been for some time in a number of countries, buyers see actual price declines from technology improvements. But real price declines are also there, if largely masked, in countries experiencing significant overall inflation for long periods. (See Figure 2.)

To compare prices for similar goods over time without going through the process of adjusting for inflation, economists typically compare the number of work hours at average wages needed to purchase the same type of good at different times.

On that measure, according to data compiled by the Federal Reserve Bank, even manufactured goods that still require expensive raw materials have become cheaper over time. In 1901, for example, the average American spent 76 percent of his or her earnings on food, clothing, and shelter. By the mid-1990s, that percentage had fallen to only 38 percent. Productivity improvements, economies of scale, and computerization all contributed to that dramatic improvement.

Consider room air conditioners, which, in 1952, cost $350 or 213 work hours to purchase. By 1997, the actual price was down to $299. More to the point, the cost in work hours had fallen nearly 90 percent, to 23 hours.

For products built principally from exponential technologies, the

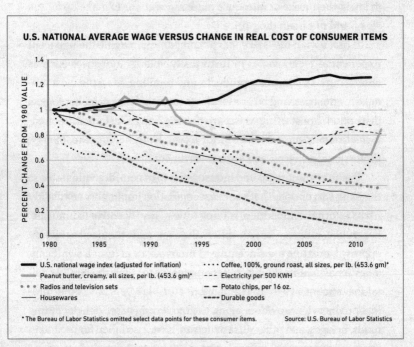

FIGURE 2. The Declining Costs of Consumer Goods

trend toward better and cheaper is more dramatic—even sudden. A cell phone in 1984 cost over $4,000, or roughly 450 hours of work. By 1997 the price had fallen to $120; a mere 9 hours. Today, a low-end mobile phone that is exponentially better (and dramatically smaller) than its 1984 equivalent can be had for $20.

Customers are so accustomed to this effect that they now expect the goods and services they buy to get better and cheaper with each passing year. Incumbents must innovate continuously just to maintain today's price. Consider automobiles. With an average of $4,000 of built-in electronics, a significant portion of the sticker price of a new car comes from exponential technology. Those same electronics, however, will cost $2,000 in twenty-four months. So automakers have to lower their price or introduce more innovations to make up for the "loss" and maintain their price.

If that's what life is like for car companies, imagine the impact of exponential technologies in historically volatile industries such as entertainment, consumer products, and retailing. Even the most protected industries, and businesses farthest at the edge of technological disruption, are starting to experience Big Bang Disruption. Technological revolution is in the air, for example, in health care, energy, professional services, and even government.

Even the most regulated industries, it turns out, are vulnerable to Big Bang Disruption. That's because regulation implicitly or explicitly limits internal competition, leaving little if any incentive to innovate. For public utilities, in fact, price changes may require regulatory approval, creating a disincentive to innovate, or at least a significant delay as regulators deliberate rate increases to cover the cost of capital investments. Heavily regulated doctors, lawyers, and other professional service providers, along with government services including roads, bridges, and other infrastructure, have also fallen far behind in adopting exponential technologies.

That lag can trigger chaos when a disruptor suddenly arrives from outside the industry. Consider, for example, highly regulated taxi and limousine businesses, which are being disrupted by new technology-enabled dispatching and ride-sharing alternatives from start-ups including Lyft, SideCar, and Uber. The new services use mobile technologies to allow customers to request and pay for rides, contact the nearest available driver, track dispatched vehicles using geo-location services, and rate the driver after each trip, all from their smartphones.

Nothing about the new services is particularly hard to duplicate. Still, instead of matching the disrupters, the incumbents are demanding that regulators ban the new services despite their obvious advantages for consumers. Rather than compete, in other words, they are focusing their efforts on raising legal obstacles to slow or stop the innovators.

The same technologies that enable the disruption, however, are being used to combat such counterproductive behavior. Loyal customers, for example, are using social media to fight back—so far, successfully. They warn each other of imminent regulatory roadblocks, and flood the regulators with comments or even show up at hearings—much to the surprise and discomfort of the incumbents.

Big Bang Disruption in transportation goes well beyond just taxis and limousine services. Tomorrow's cars may run on more efficient fuels, such as cellulosic ethanol, hydrogen, or natural gas, and may drive themselves on highways where not just the cars but the roads themselves will be connected to the Internet, constantly sending and receiving billions of bits of data.

Private ownership may give way to increasingly efficient shared-vehicle systems. New forms of public transportation based on magnetic levitation or other more sustainable power sources may come to dominate. Or, increasingly robust teleworking environments may leave roads and highways vacant, as we find better uses for the billions of hours wasted by sitting in traffic.

WHAT MAKES A BIG BANG DISRUPTION?

Today, few of the non-digital exponential technologies are anything close to a sure thing, but each has within it the potential to unleash a new generation of Big Bang Disruptors. Even the near-term outlook is getting harder to see. As Yogi Berra may have said, "Making predictions is very difficult, especially about the future."

Our goal is not to say which Big Bang Disruptors will appear, or when they will arrive. In our work with clients, we are careful not to get carried away by the hype—however exciting—associated with technologies that are still very much in early stage development.

We have, however, witnessed remarkable achievements from business leaders who have learned to spot the early signs of disruptive change and who recognize ahead of others the signals that Big Bang Disruption is imminent. This book will teach you to do both, and to develop tools and skills to take advantage rather than be victimized by dramatic changes in your business.

You can't build these new disruptors unless you know what they look like. So we begin by introducing the three characteristics that define a Big Bang Disruptor:

- **Undisciplined Strategy**—Decades of academic thinking on strategic planning warned businesses to focus on only one "market discipline"—to offer products that were either better or cheaper than those of competitors, or customized to a narrow market segment. Thanks to exponential technologies, Big Bang Disruptors enter the market simultaneously better and cheaper, and more customized than the products and services of incumbents. They are thoroughly undisciplined—an approach long thought to be untenable. Except that now it works.

- **Unconstrained Growth**—When Big Bang Disruptors arrive, the slope of market adoption is nearly vertical. Thanks to social networks and other information exchanges, customers in every segment now have instant access to nearly complete intelligence about new products and services, much of it provided by other users. Big Bang markets exhibit winner-take-all results and short product lives. So there's little point to carefully timed marketing campaigns addressed to different customer groups over a controlled product release. Today there are only two kinds of buyers: trial users and everyone else.

- **Unencumbered Development**—Big Bang Disruption is rarely the result of expensive proprietary research and development. Instead, innovators combine off-the-shelf component parts and software, launching a series of low-cost experiments supported, when necessary, by third-party infrastructure partners. These product tests are carried out directly in the market, with real users co-opted, implicitly and explicitly, as collaborators and even funders. When the right technologies and business model come together, the market takes off dramatically. A Big Bang Disruptor is simply an experiment that goes very well.

We'll say more in a moment about each of these characteristics. But it should already be clear that the new rules of Big Bang Disruption undermine much of the conventional wisdom of planning and execution. From strategy to marketing to innovation, those who succeed in environments dominated by exponential technologies have discovered new ways of developing and implementing their business strategies. Figure 3 summarizes some of the most important differences.

CONVENTIONAL WISDOM		BIG BANG WISDOM
Focus on only one strategic "discipline" or "generic strategy"—low cost, premium product, or customer intimacy.	**STRATEGY**	Compete on all strategic dimensions at once. Enter the market better, cheaper and customized; innovate constantly.
First target a small group of early adopters and later enter the mainstream market.	**MARKETING**	Market to all customer segments immediately, and be ready to scale up—and exit—swiftly.
Seek innovation in lower-cost, feature-poor technologies that meet the needs of underserved customer segments.	**INNOVATION**	Launch low-cost experiments directly into the market. Combine reusable components rather than designing from scratch.

FIGURE 3. Conventional Wisdom vs. Big Bang Wisdom

UNDISCIPLINED STRATEGY

Big Bang Disruption contradicts everything you may already know about strategic planning. According to academics including Michael Porter, Michael Treacy, and Fred Wiersema, businesses should align strategic goals along one—and only one—of three "value disciplines": low cost ("operational excellence"), premium product ("product leadership"), or customized offerings ("customer intimacy"). Failing to choose led to "ending up in a muddle."

Big Bang Disruptors, however, are thoroughly *undisciplined*. They start life with better performance at a lower price and greater customization. They compete with mainstream products on all three value disciplines right from the start.

How can better also be cheaper? As we've said, advances in exponential technologies are forging a new economic reality. Raw computing power, thanks to economies of scale and miniaturization, continues to get dramatically better and cheaper. Software can be developed in large part from existing code, and then manufactured, delivered, and updated automatically on a global scale over the Internet. Products can be easily deployed on a range of connected devices that already outnumber the total population of the world.

Exponential technologies are forging a new economic reality, but not just because they lower the cost of embedded components. They lower the cost of every major contributor to price, including parts and manufacturing, intellectual property, and development costs. By continually and dramatically lowering all three at once, disruptive technology makes it possible to sell new products and services more cheaply than the obsolete alternatives they displace.

Parts and manufacturing, for example, get cheaper as the Internet makes it easier to find and collaborate with suppliers around the world. Computer-aided design, robotics, and improved manufacturing information systems work together to simplify design and manufacturing processes, leading to fewer defects, optimized forecasting, and more efficient production scheduling.

Research and development costs are also being driven down thanks to the general availability of pretested parts initially commissioned for specialty applications, along with standardized interfaces and a move to open-source licensing for designs and software. For innovators, new sources of customer-based collaboration and funding are also available, including crowdsourced financing platforms such as Kickstarter, which completed one hundred thousand successful campaigns and raised over half a billion dollars for would-be entrepreneurs in its first four years of existence.

There is little—if any—precedent in human history for basic commodities whose costs fall even as their performance improves, let alone at a predictably accelerating pace for nearly half a century. The result is an explosion of Big Bang Disruptors that don't need to make trade-offs between price and quality, and that can appeal simultaneously to customers with wildly different values.

Under these conditions you can't win simply by making your current strategy more disciplined. Pulling back to focus on your best customers or delivering higher quality or a lower price will buy you only a little time, if any. More rigorous strategic focus just blinds you to the next wave of disruption coming at you from the top, bottom, and sides.

Consider again portable navigation tools. Navigation apps from Google, Apple, Waze, and others offer nearly if not all the features of high-end GPS devices. Most cost nothing—they're just another add-on available from the operating system manufacturer or their app stores. In short order, these apps were being used by millions of smartphone consumers, easily extended and updated through the cloud infrastructure.

Navigation apps compete with stand-alone GPS devices on all three value disciplines. They are clearly the cost leader. Constantly updated and rereleased, they have also become the premium product, out-innovating the stand-alones. By offering seamless integration with mobile-phone contact lists, the Web, e-mail, and other apps, they likewise win on the dimension of customer intimacy. No surprise, then, that after years of steady growth, the GPS device industry is in a tailspin.

But you don't need to be a software company to practice undisciplined strategy. Let's Café, which operates two thousand coffee kiosks inside a chain of convenience stores in Taiwan, is doing it too.

The company can't compete for ambience with dedicated coffee shops, many of which pride themselves on the artistic designs their baristas make in the foam of an espresso drink. Instead, Let's Café employed exponential technology to provide a better, cheaper, and thoroughly customized user experience. The company installed computer printers in their kiosks, modified to work with edible ink powder. When customers order a drink, they upload an image from their mobile device to the printer. After the coffee is poured, the printer produces a high-definition copy of the photo in the foam—the ultimate customization, and at a cost far lower than the labor of a highly trained barista.

The clever idea spread through social media, generating invaluable marketing buzz and publicity for the chain. "By owning latte art, the perceptions of Let's Café's coffee credibility and its sales went up," the company explains in its YouTube video.

UNCONSTRAINED GROWTH

Big Bang Disruption collapses Everett Rogers's classic bell curve of five distinct customer segments—innovators, early adopters, early majority, late majority, and laggards. Now there are only two groups: trial users, who often participate in product development, and

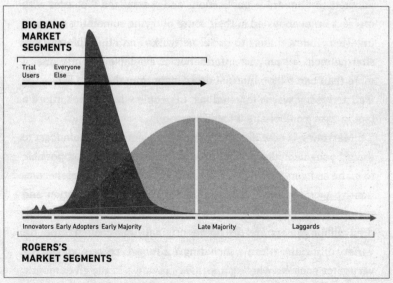

BIG BANG MARKET SEGMENTS

Trial Users — Everyone Else

Innovators · Early Adopters · Early Majority · Late Majority · Laggards

ROGERS'S MARKET SEGMENTS

FIGURE 4. Big Bang Market Adoption

everyone else. Once the right combination of technologies and business model come together in a successful market experiment, mainstream consumers move en masse to the winner. The adoption curve has become something closer to a straight line that shoots up, and then falls rapidly when saturation is reached or a new disruption appears. (See Figure 4.)

The shorter and more dramatic life of Big Bang Disruptors eliminates the need for the carefully timed shifts in marketing strategy promoted by Geoffrey Moore (no relation to Gordon Moore) and others. For high-tech products, Moore has long encouraged companies to focus marketing efforts on making the big leap from early adopters to the early majority of mainstream users, who value stability over novelty. He famously dubbed the gap between the two groups and their buying habits the "chasm."

The chasm loomed in the days when product information was hard to come by, and marketers could broadcast advertising to early adopters through trade publications and specialized Web sites with messages that appealed to their sense of trying something new and untested. Today, thanks to social networks and other information-sharing tools, all product information is available to every one of more than two billion Internet users, right from the start. When the iPad arrived, it wasn't targeted just to people who couldn't afford a laptop. Every millionaire wanted one too.

Marketing is now driven by customers, not simply broadcast to them. So segmentation, for better or worse, is increasingly impossible to manage. Every consumer is an early adopter. In the fiercely competitive world of computer gaming, for example, information and review Web site Machinima has a global reach of more than two hundred million gamers, and distributes original video content through a variety of social platforms, including YouTube, Facebook, and on the very game consoles whose game titles it reviews. In any given month, Machinima's content will be viewed billions of times.

The adoption of disruptive innovations is no longer defined by a marketing chasm. Instead, the innovators collectively get it wrong, wrong, wrong—and then unbelievably right. That makes it even harder for businesses that plan a long life for today's products and the mature technologies that go into them. All those failed experiments seem like evidence that the emerging technologies just aren't ready. But in today's hyperinformed world, each epic failure just feeds consumer expectations for the potential of something dramatically better.

Consider such captivating but ultimately unsuccessful launches as Magnavox Odyssey (home gaming), Apple's Newton (tablet computing), Napster (digital music), Betamax (home video recording), and first-generation electric cars. When declining technology costs finally make the right solution feasible, the appetite of consumers has already been thoroughly whetted. It's too late then for incumbents to jump in. Waiting for the market to take off and hoping to be a fast follower is now a recipe for irrelevance.

Instead, seemingly random experiments and crash-and-burn flops may actually be your best warning of an urgent need for a rapid change in strategy. It's like a battlefield, where near-misses signal not that your enemies are confused or incapable of hitting you but that they are zeroing in on your position—walking their fire onto the target, shell by shell—before unloading a full barrage on your exact location.

The combination of false signals and a natural resistance to change can create a lethal trap, lulling incumbents into inaction. When the wildly popular file-sharing service Napster was stopped dead by lawsuits in 2001, recording industry executives breathed a deep sigh of relief, comfortable that they could then ease into digital music services on their own timetable.

Yet earlier that same year, Apple launched its iTunes music store, leveraging it over time to secure market dominance in music's continuing reinvention. The defeat of Napster, in other words, made clear that unlicensed distribution of digital music was illegal, but it said nothing about the irresistible qualities for consumers of consuming music whenever and wherever they wanted.

Or consider electronic book readers. When Amazon introduced its Kindle in 2007, the company had a decade of lessons from doomed e-book offerings from companies such as Sony and SoftBook to heed. The first-generation Kindle was just the experiment that succeeded, providing the storage, battery life, and display technology that consumers needed, supported by a dedicated wireless network that seamlessly checks books in and out of a virtual personal library.

Amazon's devastating innovation was waiting just until the right combination of technologies was ready for mainstream use, and then used its powerful brand and customer network to launch Kindle with access to a huge catalog of books on day one. After years of failure, e-books have risen from trivial sales to account for nearly 20 percent of all book revenue. Along the way, they have thoroughly scrambled every link in the publishing supply chain.

UNENCUMBERED DEVELOPMENT

Right now, at technology companies around the world, engineers and product developers are getting together late at night in what are known as "hackathons." Their goal is to see what kind of new products can be cobbled together in a few days. You know, for fun. Sometimes these sessions plant the seeds of Big Bang Disruption. But whatever their goal, the innovators aren't targeting your business. You're just collateral damage.

In the bizarro world of Big Bang Disruption, it is perfectly rational to churn out dozens of new products and see which ones take hold. Like many venture capital investments, most will fail outright. But just one success can pay off big.

Twitter, for example, began its commercial life humbly at the

2007 South by Southwest conference. It had been invented at a hack-athon the year before and then perfected with internal users. From the start, its developers simply wanted to send standard text messages to multiple users simultaneously, an experiment that required almost no new technology. The rest is Big Bang history. Today the company boasts more than two hundred million active users and half a billion tweets a day. Without intending to, Twitter has destabilized everything from the news and information industries to unpopular national governments.

Twitter's sudden success with minimal investment underscores the third characteristic of Big Bang Disruptors. They are often born of rapid-fire, low-cost experiments on ubiquitous technology platforms and existing infrastructure. Development is unencumbered by the need for a business case or even a work plan. Experiments, often conducted with real users directly in the market don't need budget approval and aren't vetted before development begins. When cost is low and expectations are modest, entrepreneurs can just launch their ideas and see what happens.

The resilience of cloud-based infrastructure and the plasticity of software allow disruptive products to continue their unencumbered development. Even with half a billion active users, Twitter still practices innovation based on experimentation. According to CEO Dick Costolo, Twitter development teams can release experimental features to 1 percent of the users whenever they want. "No legal, communications or CEO approval needed," he says.

Big Bang Disruptors such as Twitter are often built out of readily available components that cost little or nothing to use. So-called "over the top" Internet content and communications services, including Netflix, Hulu, and Skype, for example, rely on users' existing home Internet connections and standard audio and video compression protocols.

These new tools allow consumers to pick and choose the content and features they want, competing with the bundled channel selections and voice services of cable and phone companies. And the supporting infrastructure is paid for by the customer as part of existing subscriptions—often with the same companies whose model is being challenged.

As disruptive technologies get cheaper to manufacture and deploy, innovators can experiment with new uses at little risk, abandoning prototypes that do not quickly become wildly popular. There's no need to build—or fund—an expensive network, even when the product succeeds. In the future, the most successful innovators may be those who simply happen upon the right combination of other people's technologies.

Moreover, early experiments take place directly in the market, using open platforms built on the Internet, cloud computing, and rapidly improving mobile devices. Early users become collaborators, helping design the next experiment and, ultimately, the winning combination. The most dedicated fans are increasingly recruited to fund the project, sharing in its success in a variety of ways, including ownership.

Innovation by combining off-the-shelf components has long been the norm in software, where standardization, open interfaces, and a move toward freely licensed code make rapid enhancement easy for entrepreneurs and enterprises alike. But modular manufacturing techniques and economies of scale are also driving commoditization for a wide range of parts, particularly in electronics and computing. Hardware, too, can now be combined into new and unexpected uses, and tested with actual customers.

The dramatic success of smartphones, for example, which number in the billions, has created a robust secondary market of cheap components, including displays, semiconductors, and sensors. Parts originally designed as "custom" for new models are finding their way into unrelated products, including personal fitness monitors, head-mounted computers, and even low-cost private drone aircraft. Closing the loop, smartphones are increasingly being used as the remote control and data collection device for these recombined products, coordinating their unintended offspring.

Today, new businesses can be launched without many of the traditional components of a company, including manufacturing, distribution, marketing, or IT. If the application catches on with users, computer processing, business software, data storage, and communications capacity can all be leased or purchased in real time from cloud providers. Nearly everything else can be outsourced, often to offshore partners found on the Internet.

In Chapter Two, we'll look more closely at the underlying economic drivers behind each of these characteristics. But after so much information intake, we need to take a break. Specifically, a dinner break.

CHAPTER 2
THE ECONOMICS OF BIG BANG DISRUPTION
WHY NOW? AND WHY SO LOUD?

We arrived in midtown Manhattan late one evening from San Francisco and Boston, respectively. Neither of us had had any dinner, and we knew that if we waited much longer we'd wind up falling asleep hungry. So we ventured out toward Times Square. Even late, there would likely be plenty of open restaurants to choose from, including well-known chains, New York–style pizza, and traditional diners and delis.

Within a hundred feet of our hotel, a small, street-level Thai restaurant caught our attention. Authentic Thai food suddenly sounded like a great idea to both of us, and the restaurant was still open. But was it any good? The posted menu looked fine, but it was too dark to see inside and, anyway, how much can you really tell about a restaurant from its decor or its clientele late on a weeknight?

We needed information—timely, local, and credible information—that would tell us whether, at that moment in time, we should choose a completely unknown restaurant offering the cuisine we wanted, or pick something less risky but possibly less enjoyable.

What to do? We could go back to the hotel and ask the concierge, who had likely never heard of the place and would, at best, look up some dog-eared guide or list of preferred restaurants—that is, restaurants that gave special consideration to the hotel or its concierge. We could rely on some yellowing newspaper clippings framed in the window, but it was too dark to read them and, in any case, problems of potential bias or obsolescence loomed.

Instead we instinctively pulled out a smartphone and clicked on the Yelp app. Yelp is one of dozens of consumer-generated review sites, where actual customers volunteer to evaluate all manner of product and service, anchored in this case by the familiar five-star-rating shorthand. Using the voice-recognition tool built into the phone, all we needed to do was say "Thai restaurants Midtown." The phone used our location, which it knew from GPS satellite data, to pinpoint the restaurant we were standing in front of.

As we read through recent customer reviews, we noticed a young couple walk up, look at the menu, and pull out their own smartphone. From their deportment, we were confident that they were not natives. After a moment, we struck up a conversation. Sure enough, they were tourists visiting from Ohio and had logged onto TripAdvisor—another review site, one focused on travel destinations also populated with user-created reviews—to check out the restaurant.

We compared summaries and decided the place was worth taking a chance. As the reviewers had mostly agreed, the food was hot, appropriately seasoned, and served quickly and efficiently. We enjoyed a meal that went from enormous unknown to perfectly predictable. As we left, we saw the Ohio couple and flashed them the thumbs-up sign. They nodded in agreement.

A local restaurant with no technology beyond a computerized cash register might seem the least likely sort of business to be the target of Big Bang Disruption. But there it is. In this instance, exponential technology had meant the difference between four new customers and none. And that might have been enough to tip the balance between a profitable dinner service and a disappointing loss for the night.

The disruptor here was deceptively simple: aggregated customer opinions made available over the ubiquitous smartphone. Bringing the right data to the right place at the right time, however, depended on the convergence of several related technologies: mobile computing, crowdsourced information, and the integration of hardware, software, and the global Internet. Still, the ease with which entrepreneurs can now perform that miracle meant we had the choice of several different combinations of those technologies to help make our decision.

The restaurant had done nothing either to create or to control the disruptor. Indeed, it's very likely the owners were never aware that our decision was so decisively affected by the availability of better and cheaper information sources.

All Yelp and TripAdvisor did was to reduce dramatically the obstacles between buyers and sellers trying to determine whether or not to conduct business with each other. The restaurant's actual operations—its location, its staffing, its food ordering, its expertise in creating a menu—weren't in any way affected. But that's the point. They didn't have to be.

How are Big Bang Disruptors working their magic on so many kinds of interactions, including many that may not have changed much since the Industrial Revolution? And why, after decades of computerization and other technological innovation, are disruptors suddenly arriving with such alarming frequency?

The short answer is that the continued application of exponential technologies has created a series of transformative changes in market economies. New technologies are now cheaper than old ones. Marketing is being driven by customers, not directed at them. And open innovation, which integrates suppliers, customers, and other collaborators, is increasingly more effective than internal efforts alone.

As a result, industrial-age principles and processes are giving way to radical new alternatives. Manufacturers no longer work in secret to develop new products and services. Nor do they source raw materials at arm's length from suppliers, or market to consumers largely through broadcast media.

The one-way supply chain, in short, has been dismantled. What is emerging to replace it is something far more interconnected—the ecosystem of Big Bang Disruption. This chapter explores the economics of that transformation, revealed through the three characteristics introduced in Chapter One: *undisciplined strategy, unconstrained growth, and unencumbered development*:

- **Undisciplined Strategy: The Declining Cost of Creation.** Steep declines in the cost of creating new goods allow innovators to compete on all three strategic dimensions at once. As Moore's Law and its equivalents continue to drive core technology costs down, it is increasingly cost-effective to embed more and better components in everything, even products and services far from high-tech industries. Declining technology costs have important secondary effects as well. Global sourcing and delivery is now affordable. Stubbornly high costs for R&D are also falling, as idea generation, research, and even innovation funding migrate to the cloud and to new forms of incubation.

- **Unconstrained Growth: The Declining Cost of Information.** Thanks to nearly two decades of advances in Internet technologies and networks, vast databases of information are being created for consumers by consumers, making it easy and efficient to search for any kind of information—including quality and availability—for new products and services. This advent of "near-perfect market information" means successful market experiments can be discovered and adopted instantaneously. Companies no longer need to cater to "early adopters" to establish new markets. But neither can they charge extra for the privilege of being the first to use incomplete prototypes.

- **Unencumbered Development: The Declining Cost of Experimentation.** Global broadband networks and ubiquitous computing devices connect innovators and users in an environment optimized for collaboration. New products and services begin life as simple experiments, tested with real consumers at little cost or risk. This is especially true for software-based services that are built on reusable code, open standards, and non-proprietary interfaces. Yet even physical goods—from electronics to cars to power plants—are moving to a manufacturing model based on combinable off-the-shelf parts. Even as the "cost of design" for traditional research and development gets more expensive, the "cost of combine" is going down.

The dramatic impact of declining costs in all three Big Bang characteristics is visible even in our simple example of the Thai restaurant. The smartphone apps and mobile networks that enabled our search were created on and enabled by open standards, reusable components, and app stores, a powerful platform for better and cheaper innovation. The availability of purchase information delivered on that device—reviews by professionals and amateurs alike—lowered the costs of evaluating the restaurant, and it did so at the right time and the right place (now, standing in front of the door). Finally, the componentization of smartphone app development allowed multiple developers to cobble together restaurant and travel information services, each with its own unique organization, features, and functions.

The economics of Big Bang Disruption are powerful enough to change the very nature of industrial organization, competition, and strategy. To see how, let's revisit the three unique characteristics of Big Bang Disruptors, focusing on the declining costs that make each one possible.

UNDISCIPLINED STRATEGY: THE DECLINING COST OF CREATION

According to the conventional wisdom of strategy and competition, trying to be better and cheaper at the same time is a recipe for disaster. Every dutiful MBA student will tell you that market leaders must exercise careful planning, laser focus on specific markets, and, above all, must exhibit unflinching discipline. New products and services can either be better, cheaper, or specialized to a particular segment. But they can't be all three at the same time.

Or can they? Today, a growing range of goods—including televisions, tablet computers, and software-based services for music, travel, and other information sharing—compete on all three strategic dimensions at once. The disruptors also add new features, functions, and dependability with each new release, at prices that fall precipitously until, in some cases, they simply become free.

How is this possible? The answer is found in the counterintuitive economics of exponential technologies. As computing and other costs continue to fall, it becomes ever cheaper to embed digital components into new products and services. In a more indirect way, the same technologies are also reducing the internal cost of innovation, lowering the price of producing new goods.

Combining smaller but more powerful parts with lower costs of production and cheaper research and development means new products and services can enter the market both better and cheaper than existing offerings. With all types of costs being driven lower, in other words, you can invest in innovation and still sell the resulting product cheaper than its predecessor. Innovators can offer premium products at lower prices to all (or nearly all) market segments from the start.

The transformation of strategy isn't just happening in high-tech industries. Most businesses now differentiate their wares by adding computing intelligence and information services. As they do, every industry approaches the strange behavior of consumer electronics, where both rapid improvement and declining price has been the norm for decades.

As we noted in Chapter One, computing gets predictably faster, smaller, and cheaper all the time. It has continued doubling its price and performance every few years for nearly half a century. There's no end in sight to this remarkable phenomenon, the best example of what we call exponential technology.

The key to Moore's Law is miniaturization. Shrinking the size of each transistor on a semiconductor (or "chip") improves performance by reducing the distance that electrons need to travel to execute the instructions of computer software, making computers faster and

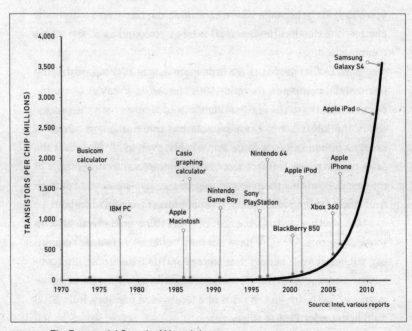

FIGURE 5. The Exponential Growth of Moore's Law

more energy efficient. New chips of roughly the same size, at the same time, cost less per circuit for raw materials, fabrication, and shipping. So reducing the size of each circuit translates simultaneously to both better performance and lower price.

Moore's Law also relies on the economies of scale inherent in chip manufacturing. While the marginal cost of raw materials for each chip (including silicon, the most abundant resource on earth) is relatively low, the cost of new fabrication facilities can run to billions of dollars. The amortized cost of new facilities, therefore, dominates the actual price a manufacturer will charge for each chip. The more chips customers buy from the same plant, the faster the unit cost declines.

Doubling a small number, as Figure 5 makes clear, has a trivial impact. But keep doubling it for several generations, as anyone who has ever mastered the genius of compound interest can tell you, and you soon reach the stage where each doubling represents a dramatic change, one that has the potential to be as profound as all the others combined.

To make that proposition a little more concrete, compare the first commercial computer, the mid-1950s Univac, to today's computing devices. Thanks to the regular doublings of Moore's Law, the processor in the latest home game console has the equivalent power of nearly a billion Univacs. More remarkably, even in 1950s dollars the price of that many Univacs would exceed the total money supply of the world. Powering them would require massive amounts of energy. And storing them would require a space larger than all of Iceland.

Moore's Law deflates the cost of everything made from or with semiconductors. We now have not only better and cheaper computing, but better and cheaper data storage and data transport. Improvements in computer memory, increasingly sold as solid state or "flash memory," have driven the price of a terabyte of memory from $100 million to under $100 in thirty years.

Data networks, meanwhile, which transmitted information at

19.2 kilobits per second in the early 1990s, are rapidly accelerating toward gigabit-per-second speeds—an improvement of five orders of magnitude. The cost of data transit in the United States between 1998 and 2013 has also collapsed, from $1,200 per megabit to just $1.57. No surprise that in 2012 mobile data traffic in the United States reached

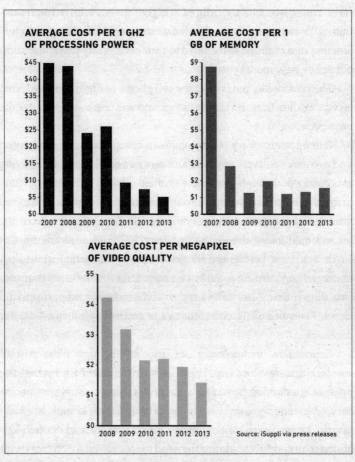

FIGURE 6. Declining Cost of Smartphone Components

nearly 1.5 trillion megabytes, an almost 70 percent increase over the previous year.

While the impact of Moore's Law is most obvious in the falling prices for computers, communications, and consumer electronics, the costs of embedding computing power into other products has been falling too. Five years ago, we bought a color printer for $200. We recently replaced it with a new model from the same manufacturer, which was smaller, printed at higher speeds with better resolution, allowed more color combinations, and included a wireless antenna that eliminated the need to connect it to any particular computer. The new model cost $100.

The cost for key parts in a new cell phone, as Figure 6 shows, cost less today than they did ten years ago, and will cost even less after the next cycle.

Indeed, technology is driving down costs across the production and delivery life cycle of goods and services of all types. Labor costs are reduced through computer-enabled global outsourcing. Raw materials costs are falling through digitally improved siting and mining technologies—mining company Rio Tinto's driverless trucks, for example, have already hauled over 100 million metric tons of earth. Sales, marketing, and service are made more efficient through online selling, turning some brick-and-mortar retailers into unprofitable showrooms. After-sales support and service are migrating to the cloud. Even financing costs, thanks to global capital markets, are declining.

Exponential technologies are also driving down the cost of research and development. Typically these costs, which include the price of conducting basic research, prototyping, and, where necessary, obtaining regulatory approval before market launch, are built into the price of each unit of the new goods that are sold. So developers must be careful to balance the need to recover research costs with the need to attract new customers. If the new offering is a big hit and millions of units are sold, recovering research costs will be easy. But to ensure the big hit, it often makes sense to charge a lower price at first to stimulate new markets, foregoing early profits.

For many enterprises, that's a delicate balance, and a risk that's hard to predict or to hedge. Fortunately, such pricing trade-offs are increasingly unnecessary. The same exponential technology drivers that are deflating the cost of components embedded in new products and services are also driving down the cost of basic research, from inception to product launch.

Has innovation really become that cheap? Consider the three main costs of innovation for most organizations, and how each is being transformed in the world of better and cheaper:

Idea Generation—Instead of relying exclusively on internal sources for innovation, companies are increasingly making use of information services, including social media, to crowdsource idea generation. In science and applied research fields, "open source" innovation, mimicking the long-standing trend in software development, has become the norm. Expensive professional journals are giving way to free Web-based alternatives. Some allow open posting and require free licensing of ideas and other intellectual property shared among a community of scholars—or anyone else.

InnoCentive, for example, runs a business-to-business exchange where companies can post their difficult research problems to wide-ranging, interdisciplinary teams of virtual experts who bid their best price to solve those problems. Since its founding in 2001, the company has registered almost three hundred thousand problem solvers in nearly two hundred countries. Companies have awarded millions of dollars in more than fifteen hundred successful projects. Using such exchanges is cheaper than hiring the experts as employees, and can lead to more and better ideas from which to choose.

Less formal mechanisms are also proliferating. In the growing community of consumers using 3-D printing devices, designs are regularly shared by users in forums hosted by manufacturers, such as MakerBot's Thingiverse. Recently, a virtual team of researchers at Harvard University and the University of Illinois successfully designed a 3-D printed battery about the size of a grain of sand— small enough to be printed directly inside a 3-D printed hearing aid.

The falling price of interaction means that research can more often be performed by whoever is best suited or most motivated to do so. Increasingly, customers, especially early users, finish product designs and fine-tune the development of new services.

Technology products manufacturer Belkin has long involved customers in product design, and not just through focus groups and beta testing. In launching the WeMo, for example, the company took advantage of the power of the crowd in a remarkable way. WeMo is a simple, user-programmable device that adds digital cameras, switches, and sensors to create "intelligent" home networks that respond to remote commands and external data triggers.

Rather than pre-script the possible events and triggers, WeMo product developers point customers to a free visual programming service called "If This Then That" (IFTTT), which lets them design their own "recipes" for their WeMos. One novel use, for example, is a recipe that checks the Internet for the time of each day's sunrise and sunset, and uses that information to automatically turn a lamp plugged into the WeMo on and off. Another sends the user an e-mail message when a WeMo motion sensor detects that the cat has used the litter box.

WeMo users not only determine what the devices can do, but can share their recipes with other IFTTT users. Belkin doesn't try to control the process in any way. Instead, product managers closely monitor the IFTTT bulletin boards to see which recipes are most often being shared. The company then highlights the best ideas via social media services, such as Tumblr.

Research and Development—Forming virtual and often temporary research teams has become easier than ever. Thanks to cloud-based collaboration services and the proliferation of open-source and royalty-free application interfaces, teams can form quickly around a particular problem, develop a working design, and then disperse, leaving development and marketing to organizations better suited to those tasks.

Incubators and accelerators have long existed at the borders of leading research institutions, but more than a decade into the Internet revolution, these organizations have found new purpose and methodologies that can quickly create successful products, services, or companies. Y Combinator, launched in 2005, brings entrepreneurs in-house for three-month intensive mentoring and development "classes." Its approach has proven wildly successful, launching companies that include Reddit (social news), Dropbox (cloud storage), and Airbnb (peer-to-peer room rentals). Seventy-two percent of its start-ups have raised significant funding following graduation or "Demo Day." (Y Combinator takes a 6 percent equity stake in the start-ups it launches.)

Even more transient forms of collaboration can be fruitful in a world of off-the-shelf components and free software. In the last decade, a wide range of organizations, for-profit and otherwise, have been staging internal and external product hackathons, in which teams of developers with access to the same tools and raw materials work on the same problem for a limited period of time, often just a day and a night.

Funding and Compensation—The funding of innovation has also become cheaper thanks to exponential technologies. In the last few years, new forms of technology-enabled sponsorship and investment have emerged, making it possible for small companies and even individuals to develop Big Bang Disruptors, without having to rely on expensive capital markets.

The best known of these new funding platforms is Kickstarter, which was born out of the frustration its founders experienced trying to determine ahead of time if their proposed art projects would find enough buyers to break even. Entrepreneurs of all kinds can now create Kickstarter campaigns and solicit "pledges" from communities of backers. If the target amount is reached, the project is funded, and the pledges are collected. Proposed products span the range of human activity, from gadgets to films, books, and even food.

As with charity fund-raising, backers don't actually invest in the company or the product. Instead, in exchange for their contribution, campaigns offer increasingly valuable premiums. Depending on the level of pledge, premiums may include pre-release or final versions of the actual product all the way up to participation in launch events.

Even with contributions starting as low as a few dollars, there is serious money available from the crowd. Since 2009, Kickstarter has successfully raised $622 million for more than forty-one thousand funded projects. In 2013, developers of the Pebble, a networked, programmable wristwatch with a special low-power LCD display, made Kickstarter history by raising over $10 million from nearly seventy thousand backers—all in just three weeks.

Kickstarter is one of many Big Bang Disruptors blurring the lines between trial users, developers, and investors. Some services even engage contributors in the process of product design and testing. Peer-to-peer lending services, including Prosper and Zopa, have raised hundreds of millions of dollars that are loaned to individuals and small businesses.

Beyond contributing small sums to start-ups in exchange for premiums, entrepreneurs are also finding new ways to take on actual investors outside of traditional capital markers. Recognizing the potential of crowdsourced investing to accelerate innovation, U.S. lawmakers passed legislation in 2012 exempting capital campaigns seeking less than $1 million per year from SEC and other regulation that would otherwise divert money meant for innovation to legal and filing fees. Though the law doesn't allow average consumers to invest in such limited campaigns until 2014, start-ups can already use the simplified process to solicit pre-certified investors with assets over $1 million.

In the United Kingdom, where individual consumers can already invest in start-ups, crowdfunding has moved from premium-based pledges to actual equity investment. Services such as Crowdcube are making it easy for entrepreneurs to develop a pitch page, offering to sell a percentage of their start-up if funding reaches a target amount. The site has helped almost fifty companies in every stage of development raise over $15 million from some forty thousand individual investors.

UNCONSTRAINED GROWTH: THE DECLINING COST OF INFORMATION

We have just seen how the declining costs for exponential technologies drive the undisciplined strategy of better and cheaper. But what accounts for the sudden adoption of Big Bang Disruptors across market segments—the characteristic we referred to as unconstrained growth?

Unconstrained growth is the result of large databases of standardized information on marketing, sales, and other transaction data, that is sometimes referred to as "big data." While big data is often seen as a powerful tool with which businesses can refine product development, marketing, production, and pricing, it is equally valuable to consumers. According to research from IDC, Internet users created and shared nearly two trillion gigabytes of data in 2011, a ninefold increase over the previous five years.

As information sources about products and services are enhanced to capture user feedback, product performance, and comparisons of features, prices, and service, consumers use the Internet to shop with greater knowledge and therefore greater advantage. They can research, select, and respond to products and services with increased efficiency, giving them the ability to "pull" the market rather than having products, services, and advertising pushed onto them. Big data has given consumers remarkable new leverage—the leverage of near-perfect market information.

However they do their buying, consumers no longer have any excuse for making an uninformed purchase, whether of major assets such as real estate and durable goods or of everyday transactions including restaurants and service providers. It's easy to discover what friends, relatives, and like-minded consumers really think of the things you buy, either through review sites or social media services such as Facebook, Twitter, Tumblr, and user-moderated message boards.

Information barriers keeping consumers from determining price, availability, or the quality of goods and of post-sales support have also been disrupted. Companies can't easily hide behind slick marketing campaigns or the strength of established brands. Each product lives or dies on its own merits, including that of its customer service, and its fate is determined not in the past or future, but right now.

There's no longer a significant risk of paying a premium price for a product that isn't worth it, or of delaying a buying decision longer than necessary because you're not sure if the features, price, or timing is right. The cost of search has fallen below the cost of regret.

To understand how near-perfect market information works, we need to travel back in time to 1931, when an undergraduate student from the London School of Economics named Ronald Coase made a life-changing visit to the United States.

Only twenty years old, Coase had a revolutionary agenda. Struggling to reconcile the socialism of his youth with the free market orientation of his professors, Coase saw big companies as proof that centrally managed activities could work on a large scale. If he could learn how big companies did it, Coase imagined, then perhaps the lessons could be applied to big governments as well.

Oddly enough, no one had ever asked why companies existed, and certainly no one had ever thought to ask the people who were running them. So Coase did just that. What he learned left him deeply skeptical about his faith in socialism. More important, it led to the publication of an article that changed economic thinking forever, contributing to Coase's Nobel Prize in Economics sixty years later. (Coase died in 2013, at the age of 102.)

Companies were getting bigger, Coase discovered, because markets were too expensive for the kind of repeated, high-volume activity that went into making cars and other complicated goods. In the market, buyers and sellers had to find each other, and then negotiate deals and consummate them. There were costs, in other words, not only to whatever was being bought or sold but also to the activity of buying or selling it. None of this activity was especially easy, much less free.

Coase called the price of doing a deal its "transaction cost." The existence of transaction costs, he believed, explained why companies were internalizing more and more activities, especially repeated functions like buying raw materials and marketing. The firm was cheaper than the market.

Or at least it used to be. Over the last two decades, near-perfect market information has dramatically reduced transaction costs across the board, from the costs of marketing to determining credit-worthiness. For more complicated transactions, it has made it cheaper to negotiate detailed proposals, purchase orders, insurance, contracts, and other documents. But in particular, near-perfect market information has lowered the cost of search—of buyers finding just the right goods from just the right sellers at just the right time, place, and price.

The source of this reversal, once again, is exponential technologies, including large-scale computing networks, cloud-based databases and software, and ubiquitous mobile devices. As new data sources for products, services, and companies come online and are combined with new tools for searching and acting on them, inefficiencies in markets for new products are disappearing, and sooner in their life cycles. Near perfect market information is lowering transaction costs in larger, more discontinuous leaps, spawning Big Bang Disruptors across industries.

That's nothing new. Even in the 1930s Coase noted how the telephone led to a radical restructuring of business, making possible the first global, integrated firms, including General Motors and U.S. Steel. But the process has accelerated, and taken a dramatic turn. Where companies were once the first to adopt new technologies, consumers now embrace better and cheaper computing products and services more quickly than corporate users. As companies struggle to retire older computer equipment and integrated software systems, some economists believe transaction costs in the market are falling more rapidly than they are in large enterprises. The balance between the firm and the market is shifting toward the market.

A decline in the cost of search has been the most visible impact of the Internet, for example, which is breaking apart many of the firms that earlier technologies put together. That's great for consumers, and for products and services they truly prefer. But for incumbents whose competitive advantage relied on incomplete information and even misinformation, a more efficient market can prove catastrophic. It's no longer true, as Mark Twain once said, that "a lie can travel halfway around the world while the truth is putting on its shoes." In the age of Twitter and other social networks, consumers tell each other everything, and do so immediately. Unearned reputations constructed over years can be destroyed in days as consumer reality catches up to market hype.

Chain restaurants, for example, invest heavily in brand awareness. The brand signals to consumers a consistent experience, with predictable if not excellent food, ambience, and service for a price somewhere between high- and low-end alternatives. But as our Midtown example suggests, near-perfect market information can level the playing field. Absent exponential technologies, the search and information costs associated with choosing an unknown restaurant would have been greater than the value we were likely to derive from choosing correctly. The potential cost of regret would have been high enough to steer us to the more familiar and predictable.

When search costs are high, in fact, some economically valuable exchanges simply don't happen. We were able to find out information about a restaurant we'd never heard of, for example, making it possible to compare the trade-offs of eating there. But there was no way to find out if, in the building above the restaurant, a master chef was testing new recipes in her home kitchen, one who would gladly trade the results for our honest feedback.

So what happens when exponential technologies cause those very high transaction costs to suddenly disappear? Extrapolating from Coase's observation, the number and type of market transactions that were once too expensive to organize will increase dramatically. The result could be an explosive expansion in economic activity as individuals safely and efficiently conduct business with each other in ways that might have previously been too expensive or risky to attempt. (Risk is just another name for high transaction costs.)

That, in any case, is the idea behind what is being called the sharing or peer-to-peer economy. While the term is new, the idea is not. The peer-to-peer economy encompasses long-standing Web-based services, including Craigslist and eBay, that make it possible for consumers to buy and sell used goods from each other. From its beginnings as a bulletin board for buyers and sellers of collectibles, eBay's digital marketplace offered a better and cheaper alternative to physical auction houses, specialty conventions, and trade shows, lowering transaction costs with a virtual marketplace that could run day and night on a global basis.

The company continues to reduce transaction costs by adding new features and services to its platform, resulting in a continuous release of Big Bang Disruptors. For example, eBay has added secure third-party payment, verified seller ratings, and dispute mediation, dramatically reducing many of the transaction costs Coase's research first identified.

The growing power of exponential technologies is making possible new applications that reduce stubbornly high transaction costs in less obvious exchanges. Consider BlueBee, a simple device you attach to frequently misplaced items such as keys, purses, and even your car—an example of what is known as "the Internet of Things." When you can't find the item, BlueBee communicates its location to your smartphone, literally reducing your search costs. The product will also tap into a network of other BlueBees and their users to find items that are out of range. When another user passes your missing item, the system will notify you. It's a crowdsourced "lost and found."

Discontinuous drops in transaction costs are also making it possible for consumers to lease, barter, or borrow the assets and services of other people. These were transactions for which search and other costs, until now, were simply too high to be practical. Now, using services such as City CarShare, Airbnb, and TaskRabbit, individuals can, respectively, loan out their vehicles, host visitors in their homes, and get paid for their unique expertise.

Historically, these assets spent much of their time sitting around when small but valuable exchanges might have been possible— possible but for the transaction costs. We may find that we have purchased items we use just a fraction of the time only because we couldn't easily share the costs of ownership with everyone else. As Airbnb founder Brian Chesky recently told columnist Thomas L. Friedman, "Ordinary people can now be micro-entrepreneurs."

According to *Forbes*, more than a hundred peer-to-peer start-ups have launched since 2009, some with funding from leading venture capitalists including Google Ventures. For 2013, these services are expected to generate more than $3.5 billion in revenue, at growth rates of 25 percent a year. Some experts believe these new markets could soon be worth as much as $26 billion.

The rapid rise of the peer-to-peer economy, however, could translate to devastating disruption for incumbent businesses that make money by mediating transaction costs that may soon disappear. The new services, after all, aim to provide better and cheaper alternatives to more established forms of asset sharing, including rental cars, hotels, and professional contractors. When assets can be easily subdivided by time and user, the value for companies to maintain permanent inventories of cars, hotel rooms, and employees may decline as quickly as the transaction costs involved in sharing them.

While some incumbents are using lawsuits and existing regulations to slow the spread of the peer-to-peer economy, others are investing. Leading rental car company Avis, for example, recently purchased Zipcar, a membership-based vehicle sharing service, paying half a billion dollars for a stake in the growing but still chaotic new market. Perhaps that's because, according to research from Frost & Sullivan, car-sharing services are expected to generate $3.3 billion in revenue by 2016.

Discontinuous drops in transaction costs are not only disrupting markets for commodity products. Artisans are using the same technologies to find buyers for ultra-premium bespoke goods, contributing to a renaissance in cottage industries for everything from knives and tools to shoes and clothing, accessories, art, and even pet food. Individual craftsmen can offer their wares to a global market with little or no investment in distribution or sales infrastructure, relying instead on low-cost third-party services that handle the noncreative part of running a business for them.

As these examples suggest, the increased availability of near-perfect market information is also redrawing the classic technology adoption bell curve. Distinct segments with different buying habits have collapsed, as we noted in Chapter One, into just two: trial users and everyone else. As a result, traditional marketing practices are being radically altered.

One important change has been a de-emphasis on the once-crucial role played by early adopters, who are rapidly disappearing as an identifiable group. In the days when customers could not rely on near-perfect market information to find out if a new product measured up to its marketing hype, early buyers had little confidence in what they were buying. Knowing this, sellers, especially in high-tech markets, often pitched new products to consumers who valued being the first to have the next new thing more than they feared dealing with bug-ridden or incomplete goods.

Indeed, the extra value to early adopters of having the first compact disc player, hybrid car, or Internet-connected home appliance was assumed to be so significant that it allowed producers to charge *more* for early versions than the price to mass-market consumers once the product was perfected. That higher price has sometimes been referred to as the "early adopter tax."

For fast-cycling products and services enabled by exponential technology, however, there's rarely the time or the need for early adopters. The life and death of new products is accelerating, translating to faster adoption and faster obsolescence. There is no longer much real value to having early adopters, or being one, and little opportunity to charge extra for early releases.

Cannibalizing your own products with better and cheaper replacements is no longer a strategy of last resort—now it's inevitable. Consider Apple's first-generation iPhone, which offered its buyers dramatic improvements in design and capability over existing smartphones. At $599, the iPhone established a premium price point for a new kind of mobile device, encouraging companies such as Samsung and BlackBerry to up their game as quickly as possible.

That pressure, in turn, has compelled Apple to offer next-generation models nearly every twelve months, not only to satisfy the market's insatiable desire for better and cheaper, but to keep ahead of its competitors, who are starting to beat the company at its own strategy. That pressure quickly erased Apple's premium. The price for an iPhone 5 starts at just $199.

With Big Bang Disruption, for better and for worse, growth is unconstrained. Either the new thing is a hit and captures the bulk of its profits quickly, or it never does. It's no longer possible to fund the development of a full-featured product—3-D televisions, electric cars, e-book readers—by selling incomplete and expensive prototypes to a forgiving early market. Consumers will simply wait until the right combination of product and business model appear, and will know immediately when it does.

Early adopters are either part of the development and funding of the product's research and development, or they are simply part of the initial product launch. There's no "early" anymore. Big Bang Disruption has repealed the early adopter's tax.

UNENCUMBERED DEVELOPMENT: THE DECLINING COST OF EXPERIMENTATION

Steve Jobs was an inveterate borrower. He realized early that developing innovative new products didn't mean you also had to reinvent the wheel—nor commission specialized parts—when existing solutions would do just as well. As former Atari founder Nolan Bushnell writes in his book, *Finding the Next Steve Jobs*, "almost all the early Apple parts came from Atari, without markup. The Apple modulator, a very tricky device that allowed the Apple II to connect to a television set, was based on our off-the-shelf design."

Jobs's insight is key to understanding the economic improvements driving the third characteristic of Big Bang Disruptors—the declining cost of experimentation. Exponential technologies have led to an explosion of off-the-shelf component parts that can be easily combined and tested directly in the market with actual users. Thanks to economies of scale, moreover, the price for components continues to fall as more innovators combine them into new things. Product developers in a growing number of industries find combinatorial innovation is both faster and less expensive than having new parts custom-built to specification.

Rather than designing from scratch, the developers of Big Bang Disruptors take the cheaper and less risky route of reusing existing components, sometimes adding only a few specific product or service elements to distinguish them. Their development is no longer limited by long lead times for designing and fabricating new parts and testing them internally. The market tests your parts before you even know you need them.

Today, mass-produced components for everything from cars to prefabricated homes are increasingly easier to design, manufacture, and source. This means new entrants and even lone inventors can cobble together and test new combinations directly in the market at little cost or risk. Failed efforts die quickly and cheaply, while the right combination of components coupled with the right business model triggers Big Bang Disruption.

With combinatorial innovation, development is unencumbered. Given the wealth of available parts—hardware, software, and other infrastructure—reuse in the open market has become faster, cheaper, and less risky than in-house research and development, which relies on strict secrecy and proprietary resources. While the cost of combinatorial innovation continues to decline, internal development in many industries has become more expensive. In a growing number of markets, the return on combine is now higher than the return on design.

The urge to combine parts and technologies in new and different ways, however, is more than just an evolutionary step in product engineering. The Internet, open-source software, and content sharing platforms including YouTube, Facebook, and Tumblr have tapped into a deeply rooted instinct for humans to collaborate with and improve on the work of others. That instinct has generated a culture of "mash-ups," "remixes," and collaborative do-it-yourselfers getting together at events called Maker Faires.

Combinatorial innovation makes it easy to prototype new disruptors, unleashing orders of magnitude more experiments, and from a wider range of potential entrepreneurs. Many are trying to solve the same problems. Most will fail. But if only by sheer numbers, sooner or later someone finds the winning combination, and launches not just a successful experiment but a Big Bang Disruptor.

This unencumbered development is being driven by advances in both technologies and globalization, including widespread access to commodity components that only a few years ago were the high-end parts made for specialized uses. As economies of scale drive down the prices of these parts, standardized interconnections and efficient global delivery networks get them into more things faster.

Consider the falling cost of once-expensive sensors. Microelectromechanical systems (MEMS), which include pressure sensors, accelerometers, actuators, and gyroscopes, began life in specialized automotive applications, including safety systems and airbag controls. As MEMS get smaller and cheaper, they are being stuffed into low-cost consumer electronics, including smartphones, personal computers, and even fitness monitoring bracelets. Industry estimates expect the market for MEMS will double from 2010 to 2015, reaching $12 billion.

A similar revolution is taking place in optical technology. 3-D depth-sensing chips, for example, power the most exciting features of Microsoft's Kinect, an add-on device for its Xbox video game console.

Tel Aviv–based PrimeSense, which developed the chip, has created a new version, the Capri, which is ten times smaller.

Like its predecessor, Capri uses near-infrared beams to sense depth and color in a three-dimensional space, making it possible to identify people, movements, and gestures, as well as distinguishing furniture and other features of a room. By shrinking the device and improving its embedded algorithms, the new version will find a larger market in tablets, laptops, smartphones, and consumer robotics. Mass production will also make the Capri cheaper, expanding the range of applications even further.

Exponential technologies are at the heart of this transformation. After nearly fifty years of Moore's Law, nearly every device with a power source now has some degree of computing power embedded into it—and soon that distinction will also disappear. A few more cycles and every one of roughly a trillion items in commerce—the Internet of Things—will be intelligent, if only marginally.

Exponential technologies don't just make computers less expensive, in other words; they make it economically efficient to introduce computing capacity into more things that aren't computers. As components become more standardized and more plentiful, developers will be able, with little regard to cost, to outfit even disposable goods with wireless transmitters and receivers, sensors, signal processors, cameras, and memory. That's the power of combinatorial innovation.

In the Internet of Things, every item on the planet will have some measure of computing power and a network connection to make it part of the global Internet. Roads and bridges, miniature satellites, personal devices, plants, animals, and even our own bodies will be tagged with tiny, low-cost sensors. The information these devices will generate will make today's "big data" seem trivial by comparison.

The standardization of information exchanges in the Internet of Things triggers another important economic driver of Big Bang Disruption: the increasing returns to scale that are known as "network effects." Unlike scarce goods, such as crude oil and beachfront property, many intangible goods, such as standards, software, and digital information, become more valuable the more they are used.

How valuable? According to the calculation of networking pioneer Robert Metcalfe, the value of network goods increase as a factor of the number of connected nodes they contain. As Metcalfe put it, the value of a network is the square of the number of its uses.

To understand Metcalfe's Law, imagine a network of just one telephone. Without anyone to call, its value is essentially zero. But add a second phone, and each person can call the other, meaning two new connections were added with one extra phone. Each additional phone thereafter doubles the number of potential calls that can be made. (Add the possibility of three-way and conference calling, and network value increases even faster.)

The best example of Metcalfe's Law, of course, is the Internet, a set of unified data transit and access protocols that bind together nearly every computing device in the world into a single, seamless network. The more computing devices that are connected, the more valuable those protocols become, driving an organic standardization and convergence that has already brought together once-separate networks for telephone, television, and data communications.

While a small network of devices is of limited value, a network of billions of them sharing information in digital form is, as we now know, immeasurable. According to Cisco, nearly nine billion devices currently share information using the Internet's nonproprietary, open standards.

In the future, as billions or even trillions of new devices share data with each other, Metcalfe's Law will produce network effects of unprecedented size and value. Anticipating continuing cycles of better and cheaper, in fact, the current Internet numbering standard has the capacity to uniquely identify 2^{128}—or 340 undecillion devices.

Network effects aside, combining is by its nature inexpensive, and getting cheaper all the time. As opposed to custom-designed parts, off-the-shelf components are pretested, and they benefit in price from economies of scale. A growing trend toward modular design over the last few decades has made it easier for manufacturers of other products, including appliances and other durable goods, to offer customized versions for different markets.

For Siemens, modularization has made it possible to outsource all but the core components of large wind turbines, simplifying manufacturing to the point where no factory is even needed to assemble the finished product. Appliance maker Electrolux, which has been modularizing across product lines since 2009, anticipates its efforts will cut the time from new product idea to launch by 30 percent.

With combinatorial innovation, designers can also cobble together a production pipeline and provide their product at whatever scale the market demands. This is relatively easy for software-driven goods that never take physical form, but the return on combinatorial innovation is also growing for manufactured goods. For its 2013 Galaxy S4 smartphone, for example, Samsung planned for the sale of one hundred million units, absorbing so much of the worldwide capacity of display and chip producers that it may affect the ability of rivals including Apple to maintain the schedule for their next-generation products. Control of component production is becoming the new competitive battleground.

Not all industries, however, are as closely tied to exponential technologies. For enterprises with research costs that do not decline dramatically, the potential for combinatorial innovation remains largely unexplored. Incumbents and entrepreneurs are still stuck with innovation by design.

The pharmaceuticals and biotech industries, for example, benefit as everyone else does from cheaper technology components and the ability to syndicate research and development as transaction costs fall. Still, given the comparatively massive costs of custom design, testing, and approval for new drugs, treatments, and medical therapies, these productivity improvements have had little impact on consumer prices for many new medical products.

In these industries, disruptive innovation still arrives in the older form of better, but by no means cheaper, new products and services. In pharmaceuticals, research and development efficiency, measured by the number of new drugs brought to market, has actually declined relative to the amount of money invested. Some in the industry refer to this phenomenon as Eroom's Law—literally and figuratively, Moore's Law backward. (See Figure 7.)

In many industries operating under Eroom's Law, the unavailability of combinatorial innovations is not so much technological as it is regulatory. While regulation plays a role in the development of most consumer goods and services, legal rules don't often stop

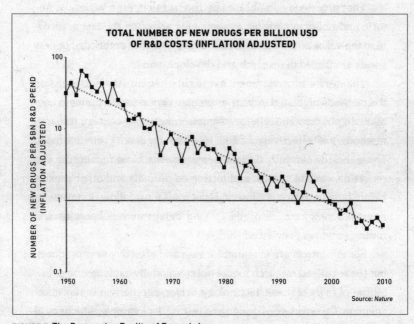

FIGURE 7. The Depressing Reality of Eroom's Law

high-tech and consumer electronics products from reaching their customers.

That's not the case in heavily regulated industries, where the cost and other limits imposed by regulation loom large in the design, testing, and deployment of new innovations. Companies that produce foods, drugs, energy, and automobiles, for example, along with professional services such as education, medicine, and law, require regulatory approval *before* introducing new products and services, or before substantially modifying existing offerings.

At the extreme, industries regulated as public utilities—closer to government agencies than private enterprises—must first obtain permission just to experiment with new technologies. They also need approval to pass the cost of research and development projects along to ratepayers.

That process is complicated by the fact that, for a variety of historic and political reasons, governments are often the last to recognize the value of disruptive technologies, whether embedded in new goods or utilized in research and development.

The degree of government oversight often translates to limits on the methods regulated industries employ to pursue disruptive innovation. In pharmaceuticals, for example, nineteenth-century research methods are effectively baked into the regulatory environment. These include carefully designed experiments, close monitoring and reporting, control groups, and testing on animals and other proxies before human testing is allowed. Drug trials must follow government-approved protocols, resulting in long delays as regulators review findings and peer-reviewed studies.

Some controls are essential for safe and effective new products, but the regulated research model unintentionally excludes the possibilities of more efficient, technology-driven alternatives in risk management. Crowdsourced design and testing, for example, which could speed the development and release of new drugs with lifesaving consequences, are effectively banned. Whether they want to or not, regulated industries must continue to design rather than combine.

Regulated industries, at the same time, appear to be protected from Big Bang Disruption. The very same rules that constrain the speed and nature of innovation in these industries also make it difficult for new entrants to disrupt the incumbents, regardless of the quality of their innovations. Banks must be licensed, drugs must be approved, and new vehicles must be proven safe. Heavily regulated industries cannot, in some sense, be disrupted regardless of new technologies that become suddenly available.

But executives who rely on regulatory costs as barriers to more efficient forms of research and development are lulling themselves into a dangerous slumber. In health care, finance, energy, and other heavily regulated industries, consumer pressure for Big Bang Disruption is building to dangerous levels.

In every field in which research and development costs are governed by Eroom's Law, there is already parallel experimentation going on based on the open, user-funded, crowdsourced tools and techniques that have become the norm for high-tech products and services. Although the practice of medicine is still a highly restricted profession, for example, health and fitness monitoring technologies are being launched around the closed borders of the health care industry, searching for gaps in the rules that can be forced open with Big Bang Disruptors.

Often such experiments skirt the law, or openly ignore it. The AIDS epidemic, for example, has pushed advocates to demand more streamlined drug testing and early human trials sooner. The life-extending potential of other disruptive technologies, including cloning and stem cells, has likewise generated growing demands for faster and more efficient processes.

Increasingly, it is consumers who are taking up the charge and demanding more open approaches. Whether or not they understand the economics of combinatorial innovation, users have become conditioned to believe that technology has created better ways of doing things. There is also growing concern that some regulations designed to protect consumers have erected unnecessary barriers to innovation. Many believe that better and cheaper products are more likely and possible through combinatorial innovation than from traditional design. If they are wrong in that belief, it is usually only a matter of timing.

A few more cycles of exponential technology improvement and they'll certainly be right. Meanwhile, pent-up demand is already attracting entrepreneurs, who are launching experiments at the regulated edges of markets as different as taxicabs, health care, and alternative fuel. Sooner or later, they'll deliver Big Bang Disruptors in spite of regulations prohibiting them.

When that happens, it will be too late for incumbents to respond effectively. Regulators will be left unable to justify limits that no longer have economic, social, or political rationales. The devastation, when it comes, will be that much more dramatic.

As we'll see in the next chapter, the greater the pressure, the bigger the bang.

CHAPTER 3
THE SHARK FIN
THE PINBALL OR THE FLIPPER?

To understand the new life cycle of Big Bang Disruption, it helps to look back to one of the first industries to experience its devastating effects. Consider the storied past of coin-operated pinball machines, a historic amusement technology that evokes intense nostalgia for many people of a certain age (including us).

Electric pinball machines first appeared in the 1930s and were perfected in the 1940s with the addition of flippers. Production ceased for obvious reasons during World War II. After the war, pinball's return was hampered by concern over the seedy bars in which the machines were often found and the character of men and women who frequented such establishments.

Throughout the 1940s, pinball was the subject of a crusade that extended to other forms of entertainment presumed to contribute to juvenile delinquency, including comic books, movies, and pulp magazines. Politicians demonized it as a form of gambling, and cities began to prohibit the machines as a bad influence on children. Machines were rounded up and smashed in large public executions. By the end of the decade, pinball had been banned outright in most major U.S. cities.

With the loosening of moral strictures in the 1960s, however, pinball slowly returned to legal status. By 1976, after a famous courtroom demonstration proved it to be a game of skill and not, like slot machines, pure luck, the bans were eventually removed.

The pinball industry entered a long, happy renaissance, fed by favorable demographic trends (the baby boom, middle-class affluence), technological improvements (the replacement of mechanical relays with solid-state electronics, digital displays, and audio features integrated through software), and a new distribution channel—the appearance of stand-alone arcades where teenagers could play in an alcohol-free environment.

Starting in the 1970s, pinball achieved technical and financial success that far exceeded the pre-ban era. New games grew increasingly sophisticated, drawing more players and more play. Annual sales enjoyed double-digit growth, peaking in 1993 with around 130,000 tables sold by five major manufacturers. Arcades were pulling in $2.5 billion annually, roughly half of what Americans spent to see movies. According to legendary pinball designer Roger C. Sharpe, "Demand was sky high and distributors were ordering by the truckload."

In the midst of this revival, however, pinball was dying, poisoned from within by a relentless competitor that started out, literally, as little more than a blip. Arcade video games, starting with 1972's Pong, signaled a gradual decline in popularity for pinball. Later, increasingly powerful home game consoles, which failed at first to find their market, accelerated the fall.

The collapse, when it came, was sudden. Only a few years after pinball's peak, the industry nearly disappeared, leaving only one company to make new machines. Game over.

THE NEW LIFE CYCLE OF INDUSTRY TRANSFORMATION—THE SHARK FIN

What happened to pinball, as we'll see, is a classic story of Big Bang Disruption, one that highlights its dramatic new life cycle. Companies that have long operated as the flippers of their industry, controlling its speed, direction, and destination, suddenly find themselves the pinball, bouncing around at the whim of forces outside their control.

To ensure your future as the former and not the latter, you need to understand where Big Bang Disruptors come from, how they enter and exit the market, and what they leave in their wake.

First, a eulogy: The bell curve is dead.

That familiar model for technology adoption first popularized by Everett Rogers, the noted sociologist, with clearly defined market segments adopting new technologies in predictable groupings, no longer applies.

Following from the work of Rogers, Geoffrey Moore wrote in 1991's *Crossing the Chasm* that successful new product introductions followed Rogers's five discrete stages, moving from early adopters to mainstream users only after crossing a sales "chasm" in which the marketing message changes from the new and exciting to the familiar and incremental.

But today, new products and services enter the market better and cheaper right from the start. So producers can't rely on a class of early adopters and high margins to build up a war chest to spend on marketing to larger and later markets. For better and for worse, thanks to near-perfect market information, consumers are too savvy for that.

With the explosion in news sites devoted to the latest gadget, service, or meme, along with social media, reviews, and other information sources, everyone knows right away when some new offering gets it right—or, conversely, gets it wrong. Markets take off suddenly, or they don't take off at all. There's little cool attached to having a barely working, overpriced prototype.

At the same time, when the right combination of technology and business model does come together, success can be syndicated in a matter of hours. Angry Birds Space, a 2012 follow-up to the wildly successful mobile game, racked up ten million downloads less than three days after launch. An irreverent YouTube advertisement by the fledgling mail-order razor business Dollar Shave Club brought twenty-five thousand subscriptions in the first week, repeatedly crashing the company's Web site.

The power of near-perfect market information can be a boon for developers, who no longer have to earn their way slowly toward the mass market—that is, assuming they are prepared for what we call "catastrophic success."

When they aren't, customer service and revenue can suffer, per-haps causing permanent damage. A favorable mention on Slate.com, for example, launched the artisanal apparel start-up American Giant into the stratosphere. In a single day, the company received five thou-sand orders for its new all-cotton hooded sweatshirt—a level of demand the company, which prides itself on obsessive attention to detail in design and customer service, couldn't possibly satisfy. "Four days later we had nothing left," Bayard Winthrop, the company's embarrassed founder, told the BBC. "We were down to the sticks in our warehouse."

Since adoption is increasingly all-at-once or never, saturation is reached much sooner in the life of a successful new product. So even those who launch Big Bang Disruptors need to prepare to scale down just as quickly as they scaled up, ready with their next disruptor or to exit the market and take their assets to another industry.

The bell curve, once useful as a model of product adoption, has lost its value as a planning tool. Big Bang Disruption has its own unique life cycle, and with it its own best practices for marketing and sales, product enhancement, and eventual product replacement.

While every Big Bang Disruptor has its own unique trajectory, the examples in our study suggest a new model for the adoption of better and cheaper innovations, one that is radically different from the traditional view of and Rogers and Geoffrey Moore. The life cycle of Big Bang Disruption, shown in Figure 8, looks less like a gently sloping bell curve and more like a cliff, as dangerous to incumbents on its way up as it is to innovators on the way down.

We call it, for obvious reasons, the shark fin. The shark fin has four distinct stages, which we introduce in the remainder of this chapter. In Part II, we will look in detail at each stage and the rules for mastering it.

The process of Big Bang Disruption begins as a series of low-level, often unrelated experiments with different combinations of

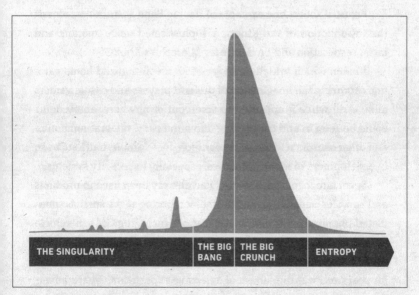

FIGURE 8. The Shark Fin

component technologies. This relative calm may give incumbents the false sense that nothing is happening, or in any event that whatever might be happening is not doing so quickly enough to warrant a competitive response.

Yet when the right combination of technologies is assembled and paired with the right business model, takeoff is immediate. Customers from a wide range of segments, including mass market consumers, adopt the disruptor as quickly as its producers can supply it. Market penetration is often nearly instantaneous.

Next, as the disruptor quickly approaches saturation, adoption drops at nearly the same pace with which it took off, leading to a period of rapid if uneven decline. During this period, early warning systems, careful planning, and the agility to quickly scale up and then down are essential both to capitalize on the opportunity of a Big Bang Disruptor as well as to survive the chaos it can bring to existing markets.

Figure 9 shows one example of the Big Bang Disruption process: the introduction of the Kinect, a sophisticated voice, motion, and facial recognition add-on device for Microsoft's Xbox 360.

Kinect, which initially sold for $150, revolutionized home gaming, capturing the imagination of diehard players and casual gamers alike. And while it appeared to come out of nowhere, antecedents could be seen in and out of the gaming industry. Integrating motion and other sensors with facial recognition, for example, had long been in development in many industries, especially in security systems.

Speech recognition, likewise, had already been used in products and services supporting hands-free computing tasks such as automated phone support and in applications including GM's in-vehicle OnStar system and the popular Siri, which Apple acquired in 2010. Facial recognition had been used for high-end military applications for years and was the subject of extensive experiments by the advertising industry.

Even other game consoles, notably Sony's PlayStation 3, had experimented with handheld controllers fitted with motion sensors. Sony's add-on device, the Move, sold fifteen million units in its first two years.

No one, however, had ever put all these components together or integrated them with a catalog of new games designed specifically to take advantage of the powerful hardware and software Microsoft used for Kinect.

The new device looked less like its predecessors than it did a technology from the future. Perhaps the closest "precursor" for Kinect, rather, was the computer interface used by Tom Cruise in a famous scene from the futuristic movie *Minority Report*, where projected displays of data were manipulated by hand motions that simulated swiping, grabbing, and dropping virtual items.

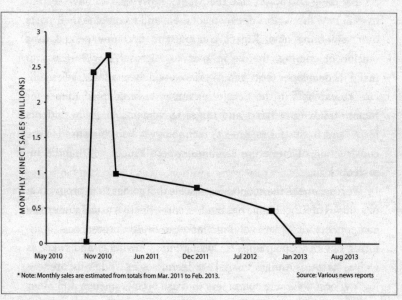

FIGURE 9. The Kinect Shark Fin

Kinect was an enormous hit, selling eight million units in just the first sixty days. According to *Guinness World Records*, that made Kinect the fastest-selling consumer electronic device in history. A little over a year after launch, twenty-four million Kinects had been sold, pushing sales of Xbox 360 consoles and games along with it. In 2010, Microsoft took the top spot in the fiercely competitive console market for the first time since Xbox 360's launch in 2001.

For Big Bang Disruptors, however, catastrophic success invariably leads to rapid market saturation, and with it decline and sunset. Within six months, the pace of Kinect sales dropped precipitously. Though stragglers continued to buy the product in peaks and valleys over the next year, the product had largely fulfilled its mission in its first ten months. (See Figure 9.) For Microsoft—and other game developers—it was time for another innovation.

Big Bang Disruptors like the Kinect, however, can have second lives as new innovators deconstruct them and recombine their parts into something new. Kinect continues to find unexpected uses outside of gaming, thanks in part to Microsoft's willingness to make its developer tools and interfaces widely available. Telemedicine researchers in the UK, for example, have adapted Kinect for remote tracking of hand and finger movements to guide patients recovering from strokes. Kinect's technology is also being used in the construction of miniature satellites, where Kinect will handle in-orbit docking.

Further afield, the economies of scale that comes from production of millions of Kinect units has made it cost-effective to use some of its components for a fast-evolving market of health, fitness, and monitoring devices. Companies including Fitbit, Jawbone, and Nike, as well as start-ups Amiigo, Basis, Lark Technologies, and Striiv, are selling low-cost wearable computers that use accelerometers and other sensor technology to track and record an increasingly wide range of vital signs and measurements, including steps taken, calories burned, heart rate, temperature, and sleep patterns.

FOUR STAGES OF BIG BANG DISRUPTION

The shark fin encapsulates the shift from strategic business change driven by incremental technology improvements to Big Bang Disruptors powered by exponential technologies. Its strange shape reflects the economic drivers described in Chapter Two: the declining cost of innovation, the declining cost of information, and the declining cost of experimentation. Together, they have shortened and skewed the life cycle of industry change, often to devastating effect.

In keeping with the metaphor of astronomy's big bang theory, we have named the four stages we have identified after key events in the creation and predicted end of our known universe. In Part II, we will take each stage in turn, describing its characteristics as well as strategies, techniques, and the rules for navigating its strange terrain.

For now, let's consider the four stages and how they transformed the industry with which we began this chapter: electronic gaming and entertainment.

1. *The Singularity*—In the big bang theory, the Singularity describes the increasingly dense consolidation of matter, heat, and energy. That state translates roughly to the condition of mature industries, where stable supply chains become increasingly threatened by the pressure of new entrants wielding disruptive technologies. Heat and energy are supplied by entrepreneurs, creative financing, and the spark of genius that locates a new center of gravity. The disruptors appear first as failed experiments that take place directly in the market, often originating from

innovators outside the industry. Though they appear to be random, failed experiments actually signal the change that is about to arrive.

2. *The Big Bang*—The original Singularity may have been only a few millimeters wide. But as the heat and pressure inside it grew, an explosion of matter created our universe, which continues to expand. Likewise, when early experiments yield just the right combination of technology and business model, they create new markets characterized by rapid adoption by customers across all segments. Users abandon older products, services, and brands, causing massive disruption to existing industries even as new, more dynamic ecosystems are formed. The old industry implodes, then rapidly reforms into new, but more unstable, forms.

3. *The Big Crunch*—After the big bang, the universe's energy began to dissipate; dramatic expansion slowed as matter moved farther along the edge. According to current theory, expansion will eventually reverse and the universe will collapse on itself at an accelerating rate. The implosion of Big Bang Disruptors happens considerably faster. Immediate adoption by the known universe of potential buyers leads to market saturation in record time. The disruptor enters its own mature state, where innovation becomes incremental and growth slows. During the Big Crunch, the industry experiences a kind of death, as value created during the Big Bang disappears. Those who hold on to their assets for too long find their worth rapidly diminished.

4. *Entropy*—According to the big bang theory, the matter and energy of the collapsing universe will eventually regroup, combining to take on new forms. In Big Bang Disruption, entropy reflects the last phase of dying industries, where remaining assets, largely intangible, are smashed together to create new Singularities. Markets may persist for older products, but if so they are likely small—the realm of eccentric customers who

can't seem to let go of the past. The remaining assets of incumbents, including intellectual property, may find new uses in other ecosystems, or form the basis for new incarnations of the business. The stage is set for the next disruptors.

PINBALL, THE REPLAY

We've stuck largely with examples from gaming and entertainment in this chapter for a very good reason. The entertainment industry lives at the intersection of some of the most volatile conditions any business can imagine. Its core customers are young and fiercely opinionated, with little brand or product loyalty and, conditioned by the industry's own products, a notoriously short attention span.

Its products and services, at the same time, operate on the very edge of exponential technology, taking full advantage of new possibilities in each successive generation of digital hardware and software; pushing the envelope beyond even where the manufacturers of computing devices and other consumer electronics are willing to go. Designers use the latest techniques of filmmaking and photography to push user interfaces to new levels of realism and interaction. Games struggle for market share across multiple platforms, including stand-alone consoles, computers, tablets, and smartphones. Pricing pressure is intense.

Competition in video gaming is more dynamic than in nearly any other industry we have studied. Published interfaces and componentized software mean there are few barriers to entry. New entrants are legion, and increasingly enter the market funded directly by users ("Games" has its own category on Kickstarter and other crowdfunding sites). New titles and new consoles tend like other entertainment products to be either wildly successful hits or disappointing duds. In video gaming more than anywhere else, victory is a winner-take-all phenomenon.

That environment is the perfect breeding ground for the kind of devastating innovations characteristic of Big Bang Disruption. Better and cheaper new products arrive at an accelerating pace, often from new entrants. When they do, older products are quickly displaced. Even the disruptors often have short lives.

So it's no surprise that many examples of Big Bang Disruption come from the world of consumer electronics. But your industry is hardly immune to the exact same kinds of disruption. If not today, then in the not-too-distant future, your customers will treat you with the ruthless demands of a teenager.

We'll look more closely at other industries in Part II. To get a feel for all four stages of the shark fin, however, let's return to the rise of home game consoles and the demise of pinball that it triggered. We'll see how a high-water mark for one set of gaming products turned suddenly into a trough, crushed by a wave of disruptive new technologies that continues to regularly redefine the industry to this day.

The Singularity—Home video game consoles, the Big Bang Disruptor that definitively and suddenly ended the nearly one hundred–year history of pinball, were hardly a sure thing. While the appeal of electronic gaming was apparent from the dawn of the earliest digital computers, the development of home video games experienced several notable flops. Arcade-style entertainment experienced many false starts and early failures, leading pinball manufacturers to underestimate the existential nature of the threat they posed.

Both before and after arcade video games entered their golden age in the late 1970s, overexpansion and poor management led to repeated boom and bust in the home market. Magnavox released Odyssey, the first home electronic gaming system, in 1972. It was too primitive to be more than a novelty, but it inspired newly formed Atari to develop an arcade version of Odyssey's most popular game, a tennis simulation it called Pong.

Atari's Pong prototype, which was installed in a bar in Sunnyvale,

California, famously broke down after a few days. When engineers were dispatched to find out why, they made a fateful discovery. Designers hadn't left enough room in the cabinet for all the quarters being enthusiastically fed into the machine. The coins had jammed the mechanism.

Something was clearly up. But early arcade video games and their at-home counterparts could hardly be thought to compete with pinball. They were ugly, simplistic, and expensive. Their designers, however, had hitched their efforts to the exponential growth curve of digital technology. While pinball advanced incrementally, each new video game looked dramatically better and played twice as realistically as its predecessor. Pong begat Super Pong and Quadrapong, which begat Breakout. Clones and competitors glutted the market.

The first real sign of Big Bang Disruption for the pinball industry came in 1978 with the arrival of Space Invaders. Developed in Japan by Taito, Space Invaders was deceptively simple: more or less a vertical, one-player variation of Pong. A succession of crudely pixilated aliens marched across the screen to the sound of an electronic drumbeat, moving faster as each row shifted down. Players tried to blast the invaders with lasers before they inevitably reached the tattered battlements. You couldn't win. You could only hold out a little longer than the players whose top scores were saved and displayed with honor at the end of each game.

Playing Space Invaders was addictive. In Japan, the machine was so popular it caused a severe shortage in hundred-yen coins. Within a few years, the arcade version had grossed $2 billion. Atari licensed Space Invaders for the home market in 1980, offering it on the company's 2600 console. Atari sold more than two million game cartridges in the first year—the first title to ever sell a million copies. Console sales quadrupled.

The stealth invasion of pinball had become a full-scale assault. Throughout the 1980s, each succeeding generation of arcade game—Teenage Mutant Ninja Turtles, Street Fighter, NBA Jam—broke new ground on every key dimension: graphics, interactivity, and sophistication of play.

Still, early video arcade games were neither better nor cheaper than pinball. Leading pinball machine manufacturers, including Bally and Midway, had passed on Atari's offer to license Pong in the 1970s. Even as video games took over the arcades, they refused to see the two-dimensional Space Invaders as competition. "Video games could not kill pinball," pinball designer Roger C. Sharpe wrote in 1977.

That's because pinball, unlike video games, was physical. True wizards relied on body English and a subtle feel for the dynamics of individual tables to earn extra balls and free replays. "There's a phys- ical pleasure to it that's much different from playing video games," Sharpe wrote. Video games were for kids.

Pinball makers were also lulled into complacency by improving market conditions. The popularity of arcade games spurred dramatic expansion of the size and number of arcades, unintentionally adding fuel to pinball's ongoing resurgence. By 1980, arcade growth was doubling annually, with revenue jumping from $3 billion to $7 bil- lion the following year. At its peak, there were thirteen thousand dedicated arcades in the United States alone. Even if each one had only a few new pinball machines, that still translated to significant growth—growth that hid the looming threat.

The Big Bang—At the close of the 1980s, the pinball business was as good as it had ever been. In 1992, Americans fed $2.5 billion into pinball machines, about half as much as they spent in movie theaters. In 1993, pinball manufacturers sold 130,000 new machines, the high- est number since the industry's postwar resurrection.

Yet even pinball's greatest technical and creative achievements, such as Bally's Addams Family game or Williams's Medieval Madness (which featured dialogue from members of Chicago's Second City comedy troupe, including a young Tina Fey), weren't enough to stop the overwhelming tide of video. While video and pinball expanded in parallel, arcade operators made more money from video games, and gradually gave them more prominent placement. The space invaders couldn't be stopped, or even slowed.

Then, from another galaxy altogether, the true Big Bang Disruptor suddenly arrived—an innovation that combined the right technology with the right business model to offer a dramatically better, cheaper, and more customized alternative to pinball. And the disruptor came not from elsewhere in the arcade, where pinball manufacturers were already watching anxiously, but from the long-struggling home console market, which the gaming industry had long since written off as hopelessly inferior.

Yet through the early 1990s, home game consoles had been improving on their own set of metrics, upping the ante on quality, price, and innovation. Nintendo introduced its 8-bit NES system in 1985, followed in quick succession, as chip prices declined, by exponentially better 16-bit and 64-bit successors. Others, including Sega, quickly followed suit. Hit games, such as Super Mario Brothers, could make or break a new console.

Still, no one could imagine that a home game console could compete with, let alone wipe out, high-end arcade games or pinball. The home consoles were little more than low-end computers. They relied on the user's own television as their display, leading to widely varying experiences. The consoles offered titles that imitated then-popular arcade games, but the sound, graphics, and responsiveness of the controllers were hardly comparable.

That is, until everything changed with the release of the Sony PlayStation. Launched with an enormous marketing campaign in 1994, PlayStation featured a custom-designed chip, "the emotion engine," that had more processing power than most business computers at the time. PlayStation's hardware was optimized for real-time graphics and simulations. With a built-in CD drive, the machine also supported larger and more sophisticated games. It could also double as a music player.

The machine was an instant worldwide hit, and Sony quickly sold millions of units. Its most popular game titles, including Crash Bandicoot, Mortal Kombat, and Tekken, each sold millions of copies. The adolescent dream at the time of having your own arcade at home had become reality.

Sony had finally cracked the code, and in an instant, home gaming became irresistible. In the end, the company sold more than one hundred million PlayStations. Longtime competitor Sega left the hardware business for good.

The Big Crunch—Sega wasn't the only business that suffered. At the time of PlayStation's release, there were hundreds of arcades in New York City alone, including the Broadway Arcade, a favorite of celebrity pinball aficionados that included Lou Reed and Matthew Broderick. With the dramatic success of PlayStation, however, the arcades abruptly shut down. The Broadway Arcade closed for good in 1997. By 2005, New York had only twenty-five arcades left. By 2011, the number had dropped to ten.

PlayStation's Big Bang had triggered a Big Crunch for the pinball industry.

Pinball, which had hitched its fortunes to an uneasy alliance with arcade video machines, was left badly exposed by the sudden closures. With the abrupt disappearance of its only distribution channel to players, machine sales tanked. In 1993, the year before PlayStation's launch, manufacturers sold 130,000 new pinball machines. Sales declined sharply starting the next year, and by 1998, sales had fallen to 15,000 units. By the end of the 1990s, fewer than 10,000 pinball machines were being sold each year. (See Figure 10.)

PlayStation was a true Big Bang Disruptor for pinball—a new product, built from exponential technologies, that offered customers

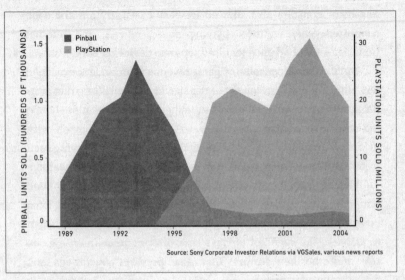

FIGURE 10. Pinball Down the Drain

a better and cheaper alternative to the core products of an older industry.

While arcade machines could cost operators as much as $7,500, for example, PlayStation sold for $299. Home game consoles lived in the user's home, and were networked. PlayStation supported hundreds of different games, while a pinball machine, even with the shift from mechanical to electronic design, could only support one basic game. Pinball machines were also far more expensive to maintain and update. They included miles of wiring and hundreds of moving parts, all of which had to be maintained and repaired by experts. Retrofitting was impossible. Other than software, most of the components were too specialized to be reused.

Home game consoles, on the other hand, had few moving parts, and nearly every aspect of game design was implemented in software.

The home consoles also allowed for easy customization and soon supported other features—playing music, movies, and Internet browsing—that had once required separate devices or services.

By 2012, home console and game revenue worldwide approached $65 billion, more than ten times the size of the pinball market at its height. Pinball machines were suddenly displaced, definitively and permanently, by a disruptor that wasn't even trying to compete with it. Pinball was just collateral damage. Yet after decades of saving itself from the dreaded drain, there were no more extra balls to be awarded.

The Big Crunch in gaming that began with PlayStation didn't end with pinball's collapse, however. Sony's real competition came from other consoles, and successive generations of home machines began to arrive at the speed of Moore's Law, offering more intense game play and other new features that made previous generations look primitive by comparison.

PlayStation was itself displaced by PlayStation 2 and later PlayStation 3, along with products from old and new competitors including Nintendo and Microsoft. Each new generation of disruptor quickly dispatched its ancestors, adding new features that made subsequent products better and cheaper than their predecessors. Later generations of home consoles, for example, added Internet connectivity, allowing users to store more of their information in the cloud. It also enabled networked multiplayer gaming, a feature that inspired massive multiplayer products such as World of Warcraft, EverQuest, and Second Life.

Later generations of home consoles also competed head-to-head with single-game arcade machines at a much lower price and considerably more convenience. The home consoles destroyed that market as well.

But the fury of innovation in home machines had their biggest impact on pinball, which had little left in its technical arsenal with which to fight back. By the mid-1990s, pinball makers began closing their doors. Williams acquired Bally and Midway. Gottlieb, Capcom, and others simply shut down. Their remaining assets were sold at fire-sale prices to whomever was left.

The consolidated Williams made a last-ditch effort to save the industry with an expensive hybrid device called Pinball 2000—a traditional pinball machine with an integrated computer monitor and advanced software that simulated video games. Sales of the first title, Revenge from Mars, were brisk, but the second machine didn't come close to breaking even.

The Pinball 2000 project was abruptly canceled, and after fifty years, Williams exited the pinball business altogether. The company took its remaining assets and focused on electronic slot machines, where home gaming wasn't a serious threat thanks to legal bans on Internet gambling. The old assets proved valuable in a new industry. Williams's revenues rose rapidly from 1996 until 2010, when the company earned $800 million and captured upwards of 20 percent of the market. In 2013, the company was acquired by Scientific Games, in a deal that valued Williams at over $1.5 billion.

Entropy—After a long period of failed market experiments in home gaming, the destruction of pinball happened within a few years. The consoles, once perfected, were better and cheaper, and beat pinball on every strategic dimension—price, innovation, and convenience. Their impact wasn't felt just at the low end of the market, but throughout the supply chain.

Stern, the only surviving pinball maker, continues to sell arcade machines for the few remaining operators. But with the sunset of its traditional industry, a new market emerged. Today, Stern sells 70 percent of its machines to a segment that didn't exist before—home users. Aging baby boomers, nostalgic for their days in the arcades, are buying full-size pinball machines for basement rec rooms, a market that, according to Stern, has grown to $30 million annually.

Recently, in an ironic new twist, pinball has made another kind of comeback. Current generation home game consoles, coupled with large-screen high-definition televisions, are finally powerful enough to simulate the look and feel of the arcade pinball machines their predecessors wiped out.

Virtual pinball games, built entirely of software, have become a popular category on home video consoles, PCs, and mobile devices, drawing millions of users daily. One of the leading providers, Zen Studios, builds new tables based on licensed properties including *Star Wars* and Marvel Comics, combining realistic physics for the movements of balls and flippers with 3-D, animated characters, and other virtual elements that would never have been possible on a physical pinball machine.

Another virtual pinball provider, FarSight Studios, takes the metaphor even further. For the last seven years, the company has been building virtual versions of actual pinball tables from the industry's long history. They approach their re-creations with obsessive attention to detail, providing faithful reproductions of sounds, music, and voices. Using simulators, FarSight's tables actually run the original software of the original machines.

The company's latest collection includes more than two dozen classic tables, which it sells as downloads for a variety of gaming platforms and mobile devices. Instead of twenty-five cents for each play or thousands of dollars for an actual machine, virtual pinball enthusiasts can buy the table outright for roughly $5 and play it as long as they want.

When customers demanded a virtual re-creation of the popular 1993 Twilight Zone table, FarSight launched a Kickstarter campaign in 2012 to cover the $55,000 cost of licensing the original design and its related trademarks. The virtual fund-raising was wildly successful. More than twenty-three hundred backers committed to the campaign, contributing more than $75,000 in just a few weeks. FarSight produced and launched Twilight Zone just a few months later, and used the extra funds to license other tables customers had been asking for.

Thus the defunct pinball makers of the last century live on, if only through their intellectual property—the only asset that can still command any value.

ARE YOU THE PINBALL?
OR THE FLIPPER?

Pinball's dramatic collapse in response to the perfecting of home video game consoles neatly demonstrates the strange life cycle of Big Bang Disruption.

The story didn't end there, however. The shock wave of disruption continued to ripple out, spreading over time far beyond pinball. Succeeding generations of home consoles have taken other unintended victims. With so much cheap processing power available in a device already in the home and already connected to the Internet, game consoles have displaced other products from other industries, including cable set-top boxes, personal computers, and DVD players.

Complementary disruptors, such as on-demand movie and television services including Netflix, Amazon Instant Video, and Hulu Plus, have turned the game consoles into substitutes for cable TV services, home video rental, and even DVRs. Microsoft's Xbox One, scheduled for release in late 2013, is expected to integrate video conferencing from its Skype subsidiary, encouraging even more consumers to cut the cord and give up wired telephone service, as more than half of all American homes have already done.

In such a rich primordial soup of disruptive innovation, it's not surprising to find that the makers of succeeding generations of home game consoles have often done more damage to their own products than to those of their competitors.

Figure 11, for example, shows a remarkable series of Big Bang

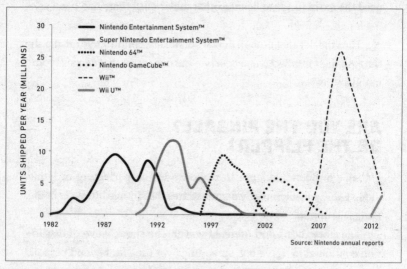

FIGURE 11. Six Generations of Big Bang Disruption by and to Nintendo

Disruptors from just one manufacturer, Nintendo. From 1982 to today, each next-generation product has followed its own individual shark fin—an unbroken sequence of disruptors unleashed one after the other by the same company.

Note how the launch of each new generation of home game console is accompanied by collapsing sales for Nintendo's previous generation product—its Big Crunch. Nintendo, it seems, is disrupting itself first and foremost. While such cannibalization might once have been considered poor planning, it has become, as Nintendo and other consumer electronics companies know all too well, an imperative in the world of exponential technologies. Once a Big Bang Disruptor has been successfully launched, the rush is on to replace it with a new one—before a competitor does.

While some of these disruptors, notably the Wii, clearly sold better than others, each release lived and died in its own version of the shark fin. The previous generations of consoles effectively played the part of market experiments for the next, building up ever-larger Singularities. When each new product hit the market as a Big Bang Disruptor, it experienced winner-take-all adoption, devastating the company's existing product in the process.

With increasingly rapid saturation, each Big Bang stage is likewise mirrored by the sudden decline of a Big Crunch. As Entropy sets in, stragglers are left to buy the once-dominant product, whose innovative use of technology has already been succeeded by the next set of exponential improvements.

Yet the most disruptive features of Nintendo's new consoles have appeared far from the world of video gaming. The Wii found its greatest success, for example, in a non-gaming application, the Wii Fit, which used sensors that measured the user's weight and center of balance to create an interactive exercise device that worked with the console. Its software tracks each user's progress and adapts the program accordingly. It even has a feature that advises other family members when you slack off for too long.

Wii Fit has been adopted by such nontraditional users as physical therapists, health clubs, and nursing homes. Nintendo has sold almost twenty-three million units of Wii Fit, making it the third best-selling console "game" in history.

There's another powerful insight lurking in Nintendo's succession of shark fins. Notice that the apparent cannibalization of sales from one generation to the next does not actually begin when the replacement product is released. The dramatic decline in sales for each product—its Big Crunch—begins a year or two *before* the next product was launched.

It almost looks as if consumers somehow knew when the next generation was due, and decided to wait for its arrival. That's true even in the case of the Wii, whose launch came after a much longer gap than that of its predecessor, the GameCube.

How can the market anticipate disruption before a better and cheaper product is even announced? Among dedicated gamers, it's not surprising to find a multitude of popular Web sites that discuss the minutiae of rumors, press releases, cell phone videos of trade show presentations, and other industry gossip. But that only explains how the experts—what might once have been thought of as likely early adopters—knew that a new product was in development, perhaps only a year or two away.

The chart suggests something more revolutionary about Big Bang Disruption. It suggests that the market as a whole—consumers in every category—were all equally aware of Nintendo's plans. More ominous still, they seemed to act as a single group in deciding when it was time for each product to sunset.

Nintendo would certainly have preferred a smoother conversion and a longer life for the older products, a preference that in another era would have been depended on adjusting the price of older products and the behavior of the company's traditional competitors—that is, other console makers.

In Big Bang Disruption, however, it is customers who impose market discipline, setting the pace of change from Big Bang to Big Crunch. And with each new generation of product, the relationship between companies and their customers start fresh. The latest innovation is evaluated with brutal honesty by the market, often well before launch. Winners in one cycle of the shark fin can quickly become losers in the next.

That new reality is a function, of course, of near-perfect market information—the instantaneous spread of information around the world through social media, review sites, and other digital information sources.

Nintendo has learned, as must every enterprise, that the information advantages that companies once held over their customers have not only disappeared but have been reversed. It is now the customers who know more about prices, products, brands, quality, and rapidly changing market conditions. The Internet has given them the tools to share this information. It has also taught them how to exploit it as a group to redesign markets that once tolerated considerable transaction costs.

In video gaming as in other consumer electronics, the days of disproportionate information advantages for producers are long over. It's not just high-technology industries that are at risk. Near-perfect market information is or will soon be available for every product and service, allowing consumers to operate as a single, potent new competitor in industry ecosystems. Soon, every market will find itself, for better and for worse, far more efficient.

Nintendo's thirty-year journey from simplistic pixilated video games to a home entertainment giant justly famous for a health and fitness product says a great deal about life for companies at the center of Big Bang Disruption.

With each new generation of its products, Nintendo has had to reinvent itself, making abrupt shifts in the technical expertise of its engineers and the invention of new forms of sales and marketing, syndicated game development, and third-party content relationships.

Even the relatively simple addition of Internet connectivity—simple from the point of view of users, in any case—meant that the company suddenly found itself in ongoing and frequent contact with nearly one hundred million worldwide consumers. That one feature transformed the company from one that sold products through a long supply chain into a leading service provider.

That relationship is expanding well beyond the world of gaming. Whether by design or accident, Nintendo is now at the center of an entertainment ecosystem.

Internally and externally, from the NES to the Wii, the Nintendo of today resembles its 1982 counterpart largely in name only. In a world driven by exponential technologies, that's the rule, not the exception. Each new disruptor mandates, if only as a side effect, the death of one incarnation of the company and the birth of a new one.

For innovators operating under conditions of Big Bang Disruption, surviving success is nearly as hard as surviving failure. So without further delay, let's look at the new rules that make it possible for companies large and small, old and new, to transform themselves into organizations capable of creating success—at every stage of the shark fin.

PART 2
STRATEGY IN THE AGE OF DEVASTATING INNOVATION

The nature of innovation has changed. It is faster, more open, and more disruptive than ever. To succeed, companies must reinvent themselves into innovators that can thrive at every stage of the shark fin, and do so again and again.

This transformation is not just about finding ways of doing things faster. There are new business imperatives to confront at every step. The unique features, economics, and life cycle of Big Bang Disruption demand a radically different approach to competition and planning, different not by degree but in kind from the conventional wisdom. The nature of your interactions with competitors, customers, suppliers, and investors will be drastically altered. Every part of the business is affected, from research and development to manufacturing, marketing, sales, and even customer service.

In the chapters that follow, we will look in turn at all four stages of the shark fin, exploring in each the new rules that innovators—large and small, old and new—are using both to produce and respond to the Big Bang Disruptors that are arriving faster all the time:

- In the *Singularity*, you must see more clearly into the future and watch for early warning signs of disruptive change coming from outside your industry. You'll need to hone your timing for launching new products and services to pinpoint accuracy, and adopt new ways of collaborating, including suppliers and customers in the process.

- In the *Big Bang*, you must be prepared for sudden customer adoption and the winner-take-all markets that disruptors create. When new competitors arrive with innovations of their own, you'll need to make use of existing assets to slow their efforts, if only long enough to compete, or perhaps even to acquire them.

- In the *Big Crunch*, you must be ready to bring manufacturing and distribution to a rapid halt when successful disruptors reach market saturation, and be prepared to divest inventory, assets, and intellectual property that may quickly lose value as a result. You must also develop the insight to know when it's the right time to retire products and services in anticipation of disruptive change, no matter how profitable those goods are today.

- Finally, in *Entropy*, companies still serving customers of older products and services must navigate both legacy costs and regulatory constraints, even as they look for new uses for older technologies that may yet have value for innovators elsewhere. You'll also need to develop a road map for relocating to more promising markets and the technologies that create them, bringing you full circle to the next Singularity.

The twelve rules of Big Bang Disruption, listed in Figure 12, present a radical new approach to strategy and execution for the age of devastating innovation.

These rules have been distilled from the insights of our ongoing study of the best practices of both incumbents and start-ups in more than thirty different industry segments. In developing them over the

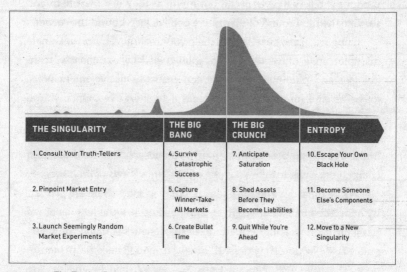

THE SINGULARITY	THE BIG BANG	THE BIG CRUNCH	ENTROPY
1. Consult Your Truth-Tellers	4. Survive Catastrophic Success	7. Anticipate Saturation	10. Escape Your Own Black Hole
2. Pinpoint Market Entry	5. Capture Winner-Take-All Markets	8. Shed Assets Before They Become Liabilities	11. Become Someone Else's Components
3. Launch Seemingly Random Market Experiments	6. Create Bullet Time	9. Quit While You're Ahead	12. Move to a New Singularity

FIGURE 12. The Twelve Rules of Big Bang Disruption

last several years, we have worked with managers in every department of every type of business, large and small, global brands and start-ups, and in market sectors as varied as retailing, energy, health care, financial services, education, and natural resources.

These are not rules that speak just to the CEO or any other individual member of the executive team. As these clear, though sometimes counterintuitive, imperatives suggest, creating and surviving Big Bang Disruptors requires substantial change throughout your organization. Every part of your business is affected—from strategic planning to marketing and sales, design and manufacturing, finance, technology, research and development, human resources—even legal.

The rules of Big Bang Disruption, in short, apply to every leader and every employee in your business.

Adopting this new approach to strategy won't guarantee you'll produce a Big Bang Disruptor, but it will at the very least help you survive the next round of disruptive change just around the corner.

Our goal, in any case, is not to help you create or respond to a single disruptor. In a universe of innovation fueled by exponential technologies and plummeting transaction costs, disruptive innovations, for better and for worse, have increasingly short lives. Once you've successfully created one, it's time to figure out how to disrupt it with another, and another after that. As new technologies mature, you must find ways to compete against your own success, if only to preempt competitors eager to take your place with innovations of their own.

While the rules and the examples that animate them are primarily addressed to executives in existing businesses, the lessons of Big Bang Disruption apply equally to entrepreneurs starting their first enterprise—which, if successful, will soon enough become an incumbent. The lines between start-ups and established businesses are blurring. Everyone involved in Big Bang Disruption is an innovator, regardless of the size of their business.

In fact, as we'll see, the usefulness of the twelve rules for Big Bang Disruption is not limited to traditional businesses. In the ecosystems created by Big Bang Disruption, everyone can and does participate in the innovation process. Investors of all sizes play a vital role in creating disruptive products and services. So do suppliers, outside service providers, and, increasingly, consumers.

You don't even need to be in business to be an innovator. The rules have proven equally valuable to practitioners with a decidedly unprofitable agenda, at least in the traditional sense of profit. Next, for example, we'll consider the remarkable achievement of two academics on a mission to settle a long-standing debate that has divided their field, who proved their point by launching an experiment that quickly demonstrated, intentionally or otherwise, the speed and power of Big Bang Disruption in the first stage of the shark fin: the Singularity.

CHAPTER 4
THE SINGULARITY
WHEN TIME TO MARKET
EXCEEDS TIME IN MARKET

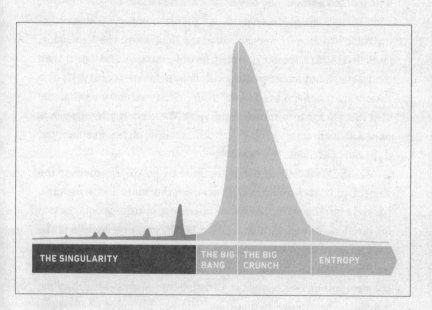

THE SINGULARITY | THE BIG BANG | THE BIG CRUNCH | ENTROPY

Big Bang Disruption is solving a century-old mystery: the disappearance of the camera lucida. Amid a wave of technical innovation in optics in the early 1800s, William Hyde Wollaston invented this remarkable device, consisting of a prism mounted on an adjustable stand. Looking through the prism at a scene to be rendered, the camera lucida creates the illusion of a projected image of that scene on the page, letting an artist trace what he sees through the prism, even in daylight.

By the mid-1800s, the camera lucida had become an essential if expensive tool, used even by great portrait artists like Jean Auguste Dominique Ingres. But with the invention of film photography, drawing aids such as the camera lucida not only disappeared but were erased from history. A myth developed that the lifelike drawings and paintings of the old masters were created by superhuman draftsmen who worked without any technological assistance.

The device hasn't been made for almost a century. Now it's coming back, in a modern version called the NeoLucida. The NeoLucida, launched in 2013, is more compact, flexible, durable, and lighter than the fragile, hand-tooled products of the nineteenth century. It's also the cheapest camera lucida ever made. Where an entry-level model sold in 1880 for fifty francs (roughly $120 today), the NeoLucida is only $30. Its first two production runs, totaling eighty-five hundred units, sold out in less than a week.

Yet the NeoLucida is not being made by any of the giants in the camera and optics industries. It's not even the brainchild of venture-backed entrepreneurs. The entire operation, in fact, consists of two art teachers, Pablo Garcia and Golan Levin, who first learned of the device from a myth-busting book by painter David Hockney.

How can a pair of academics design, manufacture, retail, and distribute a lost device in a version that's better and cheaper than the original? The answer is that they followed the rules of Big Bang Disruption.

First, they designed the NeoLucida using modern design software, and built it almost entirely from off-the-shelf parts. The clamp, prism, and flexible gooseneck mount are all being sourced from manufacturers in China, whom Garcia and Levin found using the business-to-business marketplace Alibaba. Assembly and shipping are being outsourced to low bidders in a variety of international locations.

To fund both the development and production of the NeoLucida, Garcia and Levin didn't raise capital or borrow money. Instead, they went directly to the customers. In May 2013, the two launched a Kickstarter campaign, hoping to raise $1,500 by preselling five hundred units. Word traveled fast. The campaign attracted more than ten thousand backers in its first five days, raising over $400,000. The entire production run was sold before a single part had been purchased.

What's even more astonishing is that, despite this success, Garcia and Levin have no intention or even desire to make money from their invention. They don't want to create a company to serve the enthusiastic, untapped market they discovered. They plan to publish the designs, CAD files, and even their supplier data, making all that information available under open-source standards from Creative Commons and the Open Source Hardware Association.

Their real goal in creating the NeoLucida was not so much profit as pedagogy. They want to change the way their students think about making art, they said, by making readily available a forgotten technology that once helped even the finest draftsmen create realistic images. "We're doing this," the two bluntly told their backers, "as a provocation, not as a business."

Following their initial production runs, Garcia and Levin will give away everything of value in the NeoLucida project, for use by anyone who wants it. Individuals, or even commercial manufacturers, they say, are welcome to continue their work—however large or small the opportunity ultimately turns out to be, and whatever future revolutions in art—contemporary and historical—it spawns.

Welcome to the Singularity, where disruption comes not from traditional competitors but from provocateurs who might not even want to make money or run a business, who design their products out of cheap, off-the-shelf components they buy from the lowest bidder in a global marketplace, and where enthusiastic early users supply all the funding necessary to bring new products to market in a matter of days.

While the NeoLucida itself may never spawn a billion-dollar company, the approach its developers took to bring their idea to market neatly encapsulates the new rules of innovation that companies of all sizes must follow in a world of Big Bang Disruption—the subject of this chapter.

As the first phase of Big Bang Disruption, the Singularity is the primordial ooze from which Big Bang Disruptors emerge. It is populated by weird experiments and often even weirder experimenters, who fling together seemingly bizarre combinations of off-the-shelf parts and loosely connected service providers to launch new enterprises without a business model, let alone carefully crafted strategic plans with paths to profitability. They collaborate on design, testing, and even funding with customers. Not their customers—your customers.

The Singularity is the home of unencumbered development, where, thanks to the sudden adoption of Big Bang Disruptors, time to market now regularly exceeds time in market. Right now, disruptors of all kinds are brewing, driven by programming "hackathons," open-source components, and venture-backed incubators. Their developers, increasingly financed by early users, sift through crowdsourced modifications and implement them directly into their products.

Because experimentation has become so cheap and the risk of failure so low, it's very likely that some market experiments aimed at the heart of your business are running right now. Some, like the NeoLucida, will achieve only modest financial success and then disappear. Most will fail. But it only takes one success to devastate your business.

How do you know which is which and when it's time to dive in with experiments, collaborations, or acquisitions to protect your business and take it into the new ecosystem being created? To help you answer these questions, we introduce the first three rules:

Rule 1. **Consult Your Truth-Tellers**—Find industry visionaries who see the future more clearly than you do, and who won't sugar-coat it even when you want them to.

Rule 2. **Pinpoint Your Market Entry**—Learn to separate the little bumps from the Big Bangs, choosing just the perfect moment to enter a new ecosystem.

Rule 3. **Launch Seemingly Random Market Experiments**—Practice combinatorial innovation directly in the market, collaborating with suppliers, customers, and investors—who may be one and the same.

For incumbents, the Singularity is perhaps the most dangerous stage of Big Bang Disruption. Failed market experiments that appear randomly send false signals, soothing managers into thinking the disruptors aren't ready for prime time. Yet these direct-market tests are often, perhaps unconsciously, the best sign that disruptors are closing in step-by-step on the most disruptive combinations of technologies and business models.

As investors respond anxiously to failed market experiments, the industry may experience consolidation as weaker incumbents disappear. Consolidation, however, creates another source of misinformation for incumbents. Even as customers begin to migrate away from obsolete products, services, and business models, the survivors see increased market share and positive bumps in sales. But these encouraging numbers are only masking an inevitable collapse.

"How did you go bankrupt?" asks one character in Ernest Hemingway's novel *The Sun Also Rises*. "Two ways," his friend replies. "Gradually and then suddenly."

Incumbents are going bankrupt, to pharaphrase Hemingway, gradually and then suddenly.

RULE 1. CONSULT YOUR TRUTH-TELLERS

We first met Kevin Ashton, the manager behind Belkin's WeMo device, several years ago, when he was a fast-rising young executive at Procter & Gamble. Ashton had made a name for himself early on at the consumer products giant, when he noticed that the most severely out-of-stock items were often the most heavily advertised, an inventory problem that available scanner data (which showed 99 percent aggregate stock levels) missed. Ashton, doubting the value of summary information, simply took it upon himself to regularly visit a representative sample of stores.

His do-it-yourself approach to product management caught the attention of P&G's senior management, who gave Ashton permission to propose better solutions. That led Ashton on a journey he continues to this day, finding cutting-edge technologies that can be used to capture and communicate real-time data about real things, and to develop tools for using that data to improve the efficiency of, well, everything. His lifelong motto: "No genius necessary."

Ashton is what we call a truth-teller, a visionary with a gift to see clearly into the hazy future of technologies, tools, and strategies that can change the course of an industry. His foresight into early market experiments and fast-changing customer needs enables him to predict better than anyone else when an outgoing tide signals an imminent tsunami: a Big Bang Disruption.

Truth-tellers aren't always the richest or even the most successful people in the world, but they are always the most curious. Ashton's career has included deep dives into radio frequency identification technology (RFID), programmable electrical devices and wireless networks to connect them and, most recently, nonintrusive electricity load monitoring—a key technology for future energy management. It has taken him from P&G in London to company headquarters in Cincinnati, and from there to the Massachusetts Institute of Technology, a series of start-ups, and then to Southern California's technology hub, known as Silicon Beach.

Along the way, he created and ran a consortium that developed an open standard for item-level RFID tags, and coined the phrase "the Internet of Things." He helped Belkin launch the WeMo and, most recently, the Echo system for managing electricity, water, and natural gas uses, which began life as a start-up Ashton created with research scientists from the Georgia Institute of Technology in 2010 and then sold to Belkin soon after.

And, he says with more pride than modesty, "I've never had a good performance review in my entire career."

Truth-tellers like Ashton are the canaries in the coal mine of your industry. Finding them, and learning how to harness their often single-minded focus, is an essential skill for surviving the Singularity.

We borrow the term "truth-teller" from the world of television soap operas, where by convention every long-running show has one character whose job it is to periodically advance the plot. After weeks of slow development and mounting complications, the truth-teller arrives to say the few magic words that resolve someone's moral dilemma, reveal a long-standing secret, or clear up hopelessly tangled misunderstandings among the other characters.

Think of Mrs. Hughes, the head maid on the BBC's *Downton Abbey*, who often offers essential counsel to both the staff and the nobility of the large household just as they need to make a major decision, or avoid taking the wrong turn.

Truth-tellers in business have an equally storied history. They are often eccentric characters, such as technology and business pioneers Thomas Edison, Nikola Tesla, and Alfred P. Sloan, to more contemporary examples including Apple's Steve Jobs and Atari's Nolan Bushnell.

Among truth-tellers we have worked with personally, Alan Kay has been tirelessly promoting the use of computing to revolutionize education since the 1980s, through a career that took him from Xerox to Atari, Apple, and then Disney. Nicholas Negroponte has devoted more than a decade to his singular goal of providing a networked computer to every child in the world. Gordon Bell, who predicted the revolutionary effects of a world with billions of connected mobile devices in the 1990s, is now a researcher with Microsoft, pushing the limits of personal data collection and archiving.

A list of entertainment industry truth-tellers would include legendary film director George Lucas, who infuriated Hollywood by predicting a future that would be all digital, not just for special effects but for principal photography, processing, distribution, and even projection.

Lucas put his money where his truth was, refusing to make new *Star Wars* movies until the technology caught up with his vision. Twenty years later, that transformation has arrived, gradually at first but now suddenly. Along the way, it utterly upended the entertainment industry while empowering a new generation of independent filmmakers and virtual distribution channels.

As the late film critic Roger Ebert wrote in 1999, after Lucas released his first new *Star Wars* movie in sixteen years:

> I remember a day in 1990 when I visited Lucas at his Skywalker Ranch and he explained that he'd put the "Star Wars" saga on hold until computers got fast enough and cheap enough to allow him to create any image he could dream up. Now that day is not only here for Lucas—but is approaching at warp speed for ordinary computer owners. . . . Most directors see technology as the way to get their stories told. Lucas, I suspect, sees stories as a way to drive breakthroughs in technology.

As these and many other examples suggest, truth-tellers are genuinely passionate about solving big problems. They harangue you with their vision, and as a result they rarely stay in one company for very long. They are not model employees—their true loyalty is to the future, not next quarter's profits. Their advice may not be practical—often it isn't advice at all. They can tell you what's coming, but not necessarily when or how.

"I get annoyed when things aren't as good as they can be," Ashton told us recently. "When I get convinced that something is possible, I can't let go." He loves to hear people tell him something can't be done—a five-cent RFID tag, or a single device that can identify the unique electronic signature of every item in your house that draws power—because it motivates him to prove them wrong. Experience has taught him that with the right group of engineers, anything is possible.

Learning to find truth-tellers is hard. They are often found outside your organization. They may be customers, suppliers, industry analysts—even science fiction writers. They haunt message boards, trade shows, and conferences, proclaiming their truths to anyone who will listen.

Learning to understand them, and to appreciate their value, is even harder. "Most managers either fire them or bore them," Ashton says of his fellow truth-tellers. Ashton's boss, Chet Pipkin, sees it differently. Perhaps that's because Pipkin, the founder and CEO of privately held Belkin, is himself a technology maverick, once described as "the wealthiest tech entrepreneur you've never heard of." He told us:

> One of the biggest obstacles for executives today is being surrounded by people who don't speak their mind, or have such heavy filters on all the time. I need "positive disrupters" around me. You can call them trouble makers. I do, sometimes.

Kevin's a thinker, a challenger. He gets me thinking big thoughts. Sometimes I'm not in the right frame of mind to be willing to hear what he has to say. But when that happens, it's my loss.

If you or your organization can't handle these "positive disrupters," as Pipkin calls the truth-tellers, good data can often substitute for human visionaries. If you ask the right questions, the market will readily confess strong signals of technological upheavals to come. The problem is that most executives miss these signals. We have warehouses full of data and the latest tools for business intelligence and data analytics, but these tend to be internally focused. While those techniques are essential for incremental improvements in performance, they don't work to predict Big Bang Disruption.

For that, you need new analytic tools, ones based on the external data sources of near-perfect market information. Rather than projecting market behavior from sanitized proprietary data, in other words, look for evidence of actual customers, reviewers, critics, and developers arguing—often ferociously—about new technologies, new products, and long-standing problems with your industry. They may signal excessive transaction costs that you or someone else could find new ways to eliminate.

As an example, think of the explosion of innovation going on right now in personal health care. Given the changing demographics of an aging world population and the potential of exponential technologies to resolve enormous inefficiencies in the existing health care industry, the opportunities for Big Bang Disruption should be visible to everyone—everyone paying attention, in any case.

Innovators both inside and outside the industry have launched dozens of experiments, many of them aimed at using off-the-shelf component parts to monitor and report a growing list of an individual's vital signs, activity, and general health. Every month brings new kinds of sensors, new user interfaces, and new ways of collecting, analyzing, and reporting data collected from these devices to help athletes, seniors, parents, and average consumers take a more active role in managing their own health.

Earlier, we mentioned products such as the Fitbit, which repurposes accelerometers, Bluetooth transceivers, and other smartphone components to create wearable activity monitors. Our research has cataloged nearly two dozen similar market experiments, each with slightly different technologies, business models, and approaches to changing the way consumers monitor their own bodies.

Entrepreneurs and incumbents, including Jawbone, Nike, and Under Armour, are selling devices that track activity, sleep, heart rate, temperature, blood pressure, and weight. As Moore's Law pushes the price and size of sensors down, the devices are becoming less intrusive and lighter weight. One company, Valencell, has exploited this trend by embedding the sensors into a pair of music ear buds, allowing runners and other exercisers to collect data without adding another device to their kit.

Another group takes advantage of cloud computing and the spread of wireless networks to provide long-distance interactive monitors for babies, seniors, and patients with disabilities. Cameras and microphones allow parents and caregivers not only to see and hear, but to talk to or, in the case of babies, sing to, those they are watching. A company called AdhereTech has patented "smart pill bottles" that measure the number of pills or the amount of liquid remaining, reminding users when it is time to take their medications.

Taken together, it's no exaggeration to say that these products signal a revolt against the considerable inefficiencies of modern medicine, where both the collection and interpretation of patient data is restricted to a professional class of doctors, nurses, and other health care workers. Ballooning transaction costs for scheduling, traveling, and waiting for caregivers to take and report basic health data are making face-to-face interactions with health care professionals increasingly inconvenient or even unaffordable.

Technology is coming to the rescue. So far, the innovations have been modest; hardly enough, in any case, to shake the foundations of the $3 trillion U.S. health sector. But for health care providers, regulators, insurers, pharmaceutical companies, and suppliers, these products and services signal growing demand for more information, more control, and more preventive care. They are some of the best truth-tellers the industry could possibly have of the shape, direction, and intensity of the coming upheaval.

Customer unrest is also increasing in other industries that feature long-standing inefficiencies, encouraging more of the kinds of experiments that signal imminent disruption. Transportation apps including Uber, Lyft, and Hailo, for example, can be seen as attempts to use technology to improve the customer interface in highly regulated taxi and limousine services, while Airbnb and Wimdu are experimenting with new ways to rent temporary lodgings. A start-up called Expensify is aimed at helping business travelers collect and report their reimbursable expenses, a source of enormous frustration for the frequent-flyer crowd.

Each of these experiments is working at the margins of stubbornly persistent consumer irritations in travel and hospitality, reflecting vast opportunities for disruptive technologies. Together, they underscore a key lesson about truth-telling. One form of early detection radar for your own business begins with a sober and honest evaluation of existing pain points in the supply chain, either for your customers or suppliers or both. Then ask what available information sources could be coordinated through mobile devices and cloud services to resolve much of that pain.

Once you have the list, look for market experiments that are already trying to solve your customers' problems or analogous ones from other industries. If you find some, you know where to aim your market intelligence machinery. If you don't, you found a Big Bang Disruption opportunity of your own.

Our research suggests that another frequent indicator of imminent disruption is a sudden rise in lobbying and litigation aimed at stalling or stopping emerging technology platforms. As we've seen, exponential technologies often create sudden breaks with past practices, catching industry incumbents off guard. When they do, a common response for entrenched interests is to use their market power and cash reserves to overwhelm early experiments with lawsuits and other legal obstacles. (We'll explore that strategy in more detail in Chapter Five.)

In the shift from media-based to cloud-based delivery of entertainment and other content, for example, legal battles have so far centered on calls by the incumbents to expand the reach of international copyright laws, both by banning new technologies that can be used to evade digital rights management systems and by adding new civil and criminal penalties for unlicensed copying and distribution.

When the costs of media and distribution were high, copyright laws of long duration and little leeway for incidental remixing or reuse made good economic sense. Now that information is increasingly created, organized, and distributed entirely in the cloud, the costs of today's copyright system are seen by many as exceeding their benefit. Many consumers are resisting added legal protections for copyright holders and calling instead for radical reform of the system, demanding that its scope and duration be reduced to reflect the lower costs of digital distribution and the shorter life span of many works.

Whatever the merits of arguments made by both sides, consumers have grown increasingly brazen in their refusal to recognize laws they see as obsolete and counterproductive. In a war that is taking place in the market as well as in courts and in legislatures, consumers are finding powerful new partners. Entrepreneurs and venture investors are joining forces with the powerful consumer electronics lobby to push back against content producers in the entertainment, news, and software industries.

Consider Aereo TV, a start-up backed by media veteran Barry Diller. Aereo captures over-the-air signals from television broadcasters in local markets, and then replays the programming on demand to its customers over the Internet. To stay within the legal limits of copyright, Aereo's technical architecture assigns each customer his own separate TV antenna in Aereo's data centers, which, thanks to Moore's Law, is about the size of a small coin. (Individual consumers recording and replaying over-the-air programming is not considered a violation of U.S. copyright law.)

Broadcasters including many of the largest broadcast networks have filed multiple lawsuits against Aereo, arguing that the individual antennae are simply a technical trick to avoid liability for what they see as wholesale copying and redistribution of copyrighted programming. So far, Aereo has won the early rounds in the courts. But whether or not the service is ultimately found to be legal, its immediate popularity with consumers demonstrates growing demand for more flexible programming options.

Current copyright battles follow a similar trajectory to earlier fights over disruptive copying and distribution technologies, going all the way back to the days of player pianos and the invention of photocopying. Previous battles include the successful defense of home videotape recording in 1984 (the Sony Betamax), the defeat of the first peer-to-peer technologies for information sharing in 2001 (Napster), and a successful Internet user revolt in 2012 over proposed new copyright laws in the United States known as SOPA and PIPA.

Though both sides have historically won their share of the skirmishes, in the end the outcome is always decided by exponential technologies—Moore's Law, that is, rather than traditional law.

RULE 2. PINPOINT YOUR MARKET ENTRY

Big Bang Disruptors don't succeed by accident of birth. Their developers are cold calculators, learning from the lessons of seemingly random failed market experiments. Was the technology not powerful enough? Was it still too expensive? Did the innovator lack the right partners, platforms, or business model? Was a successful experiment the Big Bang, or just a little bump, foreshadowing an even bigger explosion on the near horizon? Launching too soon or too late is equally catastrophic.

Amazon's Jeff Bezos, for one, is both a truth-teller in his own right as well as a master of good timing. His initial decision to launch the company as a virtual bookstore and locate it in Seattle in 1994, as the famous story goes, was worked out in the course of a cross-country drive. Bezos, in true Coasean style, considered the sources of inefficiency in several industries. He chose books for his e-commerce venture because of the high transaction costs in the supply chain of a product with an enormous number of SKUs, a small shippable size, and many sellers served by a few dominant middlemen.

In the decade that followed, Amazon has chosen the perfect time to launch more disruptors, including the addition of new categories of products and the integration of third-party retailers (Amazon Marketplace), subscription-based expedited delivery (Amazon Prime), and the leveraging of Amazon's hardware and software infrastructure for other merchants (Amazon Web Services).

In many cases, Bezos launched these initiatives just before his competitors, some of them technology giants in their own right. By getting the timing just right, Bezos has significantly outpaced the fourteen next largest Internet retailers over the past ten years. Amazon's sales hit $61 billion in 2012, and its market value more than tripled between 2000 and 2013. eBay, by comparison, which missed

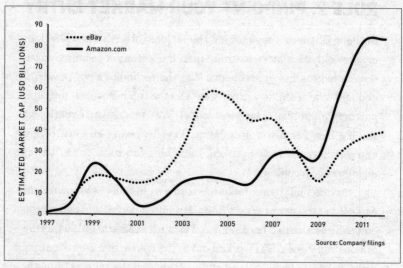

FIGURE 14. Amazon Pulls Ahead

only a few steps, has grown in value from $18 billion to $40 billion in the same period. (See Figure 14.)

Perhaps the best example of Amazon's keen sense of timing, however, is its 2007 decision to launch the Kindle, its wildly popular e-book reader. Originally priced at $399 in the United States, the first Kindle sold out in five and a half hours. Five generations later, the price has since fallen to $69 for a basic model that is better than the original.

The Kindle was hardly the first attempt to create an electronic book; it was simply the first one to become a Big Bang Disruptor. Amazon had a decade of doomed market experiments to study, including expensive flops like NuvoMedia's Rocket eBook, the EveryBook Reader, the Librius Millennium Reader, and the SoftBook Reader. While none of them had any obvious impact on sales for print books, as Figure 15 suggests, they signaled the kind of potential devastation that began suddenly with the Kindle's release.

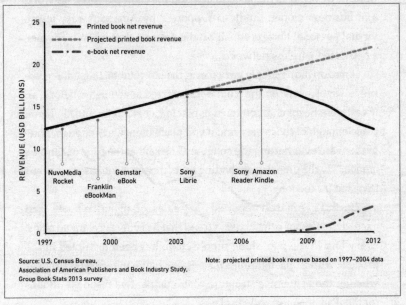

Source: U.S. Census Bureau, Association of American Publishers and Book Industry Study, Group Book Stats 2013 survey

Note: projected printed book revenue based on 1997–2004 data

FIGURE 15. Failed Market Experiments and the Disruption of Print Books

Bezos's genius was to recognize those few essential components the early experiments lacked, including sufficient storage and battery life, and a display technology that could emulate the readability of paper. Then he waited the necessary few turns of exponential improvement needed to bring the right technologies to mainstream status.

For the display, Amazon patiently watched for the maturation of E Ink, which uses microcapsules the width of a human hair that can switch from black to white with a simple magnetic charge. (E Ink began life as a research project at MIT.) Using E Ink, the first Kindle displays were easier on the eyes for long periods of time than traditional LCD technology, and used less power.

Just as important as applying the right technology at the right time, however, was the need to develop the right platform, network, and business model. Kindle is supported by Amazon's easy-to-use virtual personal library, which Kindle delivers through Whispernet, a dedicated wireless network.

Amazon didn't simply swoop in at the last minute. Indeed, according to Bezos, work on the Kindle had started seven years before, an investment Bezos characterized as placing a bet on the future. "If you place enough of those bets, and if you place them early enough, none of them are ever betting the company," he said at the time of Kindle's launch. "By the time you are betting the company, it means you haven't invested for too long."

By 2011, Amazon reported that sales of digital e-books had exceeded sales for print books, a trend that has only accelerated since. Every link in the publishing supply chain has been disrupted in the process, with Apple fighting a high-stakes battle in federal court over whether the aggressive structure of its competitive response, iBooks for the iPad, violated antitrust laws.

Pinpoint accuracy was equally critical in Apple's iPod, a digital music player that became the company's first noncomputer Big Bang Disruptor. By 2000, portable digital devices had all but wiped out the market for CD players such as the Walkman. But none really dominated the new market or expanded it beyond a replacement product. As late as 2001, the best-of-breed Nomad Jukebox weighed twice as much as a portable CD player, had a slow, hard-to-use interface for transferring music files, and poor battery life.

By then, thanks to the success of the iTunes store, Apple had developed considerable leverage in the music industry. The company had access to a vast catalog of digital music, the world's best software designers, and a high-speed file transfer technology called FireWire. It could also rely on the growing cell phone market for plentiful, low-cost batteries and displays.

A chance meeting in Tokyo with Toshiba by Apple's Jon Rubinstein, lead engineer for many of the company's best computer products, solved the remaining problem: storage. Toshiba revealed that it had recently developed a 1.8-inch hard drive—considerably smaller than the one used by Nomad.

But Toshiba had no particular plans for the drive. "They said they didn't know what to do with it," Rubinstein later told *Wired* magazine. "Maybe put it in a small notebook." Rubinstein returned to Apple and proposed a very different idea to CEO Steve Jobs. "I went back to Steve and I said, 'I know how to do this. I've got all the parts.' He said, 'Go for it.'"

He did, and the rest is history. The iPod, released in late 2001, was an immediate success, outselling not only Nomad and other digital music players but expanding the reach of the devices from tech-savvy buyers to consumers of nearly every age. By the end of 2002, Apple had sold six hundred thousand iPods. Successive generations have expanded the storage, features, and connectivity of the device. Apple has sold three hundred and fifty million units.

Beyond the iPod's unquestioned success, however, has been its catalytic effect on both the entertainment industry and Apple itself. The company dominates the sale of digital music and has leveraged its experience with iPod to launch even more perfectly timed consumer electronics products—the iPhone and the iPad. By 2012, the company had outgrown its origins as a computer company, with only 15 percent of its revenue coming from the sale of Macs.

With the opening of the first Apple stores in 2001, meanwhile, the company began its reinvention of electronics retailing, leaving big-box retailers scratching their heads and, soon, drastically scaling back their number of stores.

As these examples suggest, the perfect time to enter the Singularity depends not only on an accurate reading of the tea leaves left by your truth-tellers but on an accurate reading of the role you are best suited to play in a new ecosystem created by Big Bang Disruption.

Our research has uncovered several distinct paths companies can take in the world of seemingly random market experiments, including combiner, supplier, and investor. Amazon and Apple succeeded by combining the right technologies with the right business model. But the companies that supplied the component parts, platforms, embedded software, and network infrastructure Kindle and iPod relied on are also key participants. They make it possible for the experimenters to reach early users instantly and cheaply.

Investors, especially venture capitalists and private funders known as "angels," also play a critical role by financing the experiments—a role now being supplemented by crowdfunding services.

While all three kinds of participants need truth-tellers and perfectly timed market entry to succeed, their approaches differ significantly. The combiners charge hard at a vision, fully expecting each market experiment will yield a Big Bang Disruptor. Suppliers, on the other hand, aim to work with enough of the experimenters to become the preferred or even exclusive supplier for products and services that take off. And investors spread their bets over a portfolio of experiments, and must do so early enough to own a significant piece of the winner.

The proliferation of low-cost experiments, many combining the same basic components, is putting pressure on the traditional venture investing model. The typical venture capitalist assumes the vast majority of the companies in her portfolio will fail to ever launch a successful product, let alone make a profit. Instead, the best investors manage their funds to ensure that if only one company succeeds, it does so in a big way. These early stage investors are primed for Big Bang Disruptors, increasingly the victors in winner-take-all markets.

But the precision timing of even the best venture capitalists is being challenged by the new economics of unencumbered development. Because experimentation is so inexpensive, entrepreneurs increasingly bootstrap the early stages of product and company development, or look to crowdfunding and other forms of voluntary contributions that don't dilute ownership in the business. That means fewer start-ups need VC funding and expertise, or at least can defer that stage until the product has already hit the market and the company has more leverage with outside investors.

For Big Bang Disruptors that still require significant outside capital, investors are confronted with a dizzying range of choices to review. Many similar efforts might be heavily funded, with the expectation that only one will emerge as the winner. Today, for example, venture investors are chasing an elusive Big Bang Disruptor for digital payment processing, one that would use a combination of mobile technologies to replace cash, checks, and credit cards. The right combination of better and cheaper technologies could devastate the supply chain of many incumbents in the financial services industry.

The complicated interactions of banks, payments processors, and merchants, however, have so far translated into a long period of failed market experiments. Still, the stakes are high enough that the potential of a winning combination has proven irresistible to venture investors. According to David Hornik, a partner with August Capital, "There's a lot of froth right now, but anything is possible when enough smart people are trying out a myriad of different solutions."

Because the winning combination will generate tremendous returns, many investors are making big bets, paying what Hornik acknowledges are "irrational prices for the ones that look like the big winner." Whoever creates the mobile payment disruptor will likely experience a multibillion-dollar payout, similar to Big Bang Disruptors like Facebook and LinkedIn. All the value will go to the winner. In retrospect, all the other investments will look excessive, even foolish.

There is a growing anxiety, Hornik says, that early stage investors are committing "venture fratricide." In some sense, no matter who wins, the investing community as a whole will likely lose.

In an increasing number of examples in our study, however, entrepreneurs never even reach the point of taking on outside funding, selling their Big Bang Disruptors when they are still in the experiment stage. That kind of timing requires acute market sensitivity, and nerves of steel.

But it doesn't necessarily require experience. Consider the story of Nick D'Aloisio, who in 2013 sold Summly, his news-reading program, to Yahoo for an amount estimated to be as much as $30 million. It isn't clear what's more remarkable about this story—that Summly, which automatically summarizes long articles into synopses for display on mobile devices, had only existed for a few months, or that D'Aloisio was only seventeen years old at the time of the sale. "I've still got a year and a half left at my high school," he told the *New York Times*. D'Aloisio will have to test out of his remaining classes in order to work with Yahoo's London office to integrate the software.

The decision to sell a product or even a company during the Singularity stage is a decision to sell a potential Big Bang Disruptor to just one customer rather than pressing on in hopes of millions of buyers later. Obviously, that decision is fraught with risk for both buyer and seller. Yahoo may never recover its investment in Summly.

On the other hand, waiting for evidence that an experiment will prove to be a winner can quickly become an expensive hedging strategy. Google, for example, purchased YouTube only after the start-up had taken off, paying $1.65 billion. Microsoft paid more than $8 billion for Skype, the pioneering Internet-based telephone and video chat service. Shortly after it acquired Summly, Yahoo spent $1.1 billion for microblogging phenomenon Tumblr, which had amassed more than nine million visitors in twelve months.

How do you know whether to look for one buyer or millions of customers? The tendency of Big Bang Disruption toward winner-take-all markets with little left for second- and third-place finishers weighs in favor of an early exit, especially for start-ups such as

Summly that don't have the experience or infrastructure to see the experiment through to sudden success. Established innovators such as Amazon, with deep ties to the industry and a long balance sheet of dedicated assets, can afford to place many bets, and let more of them ride.

RULE 3. LAUNCH SEEMINGLY RANDOM MARKET EXPERIMENTS

With truth-tellers in hand and market entry pinpointed, the real work of the Singularity begins: the rapid-fire launch of market experiments that engage actual customers. The Singularity is characterized by highly transient, often virtual collaborations with developers and early users that may last no longer than a day or two—long enough just to launch an experiment.

These experiments also make use of different materials, including off-the-shelf component parts and existing infrastructure, such as cloud computing, that make instant market tests possible, cheap, and low-risk. Experiments take place in real time and with real users—preferably someone else's. Early market experiments don't produce perfect products for specific markets, but instead leverage existing, scalable development platforms that can remain open to outside collaboration.

Big Bang innovation emphasizes collaboration with a range of new users, who may or may not turn out to be customers at all. So the challenge for entrepreneurs of all shapes and sizes is learning to shift research and development from inside to outside. It's a challenge they must overcome. In the world of Big Bang Disruption, the cost of combine is lower than the cost of design.

In the new market for private unmanned aircraft, for example, hobbyists already have a robust platform of do-it-yourself (DIY) options to develop and build their own personalized drones. Aside from controversial military uses, commercial and even personal drones are poised to be Big Bang Disruptors in a variety of fields, including police surveillance, search and rescue, agriculture, wildlife preservation, aerial photography, and even local delivery. The Federal Aviation Administration estimates that within the next decade, the market for personal drones within the United States alone will top $10 billion.

Experimentation is easy when parts are cheap and plentiful and an ecosystem of like-minded innovators are sharing their designs. Drones controlled by existing mobile devices, including phones and tablets, are already priced below $300, several orders of magnitude cheaper than the $4 million military version (the private drones don't carry weapons).

How has a market that only barely exists achieved such bare-bones pricing? The answer is reusable components. Drones and smartphones use many of the same parts, including gyroscopes, accelerometers, GPS chips, and CPUs. Economies of scale in the maturing smartphone industry are unintentionally driving down costs in the nascent drone market.

The low cost of entry is jump-starting an enthusiastic community of hobbyists—more co-developers than trial users—driving new applications and a push for regulatory relief. DIY Drones, the leading Web site for enthusiasts, has nearly forty thousand members. Former *Wired* editor Chris Anderson, one of the DIY industry's original truth-tellers, left journalism to become chief executive of 3D Robotics, which sells more personal drones every six months than the entire fleet of the U.S. military. "Regular people couldn't build an autopilot ten years ago," Anderson said recently. "Five years ago it was unaffordable. And now we can buy the parts at Radio Shack."

Early users aren't the only source of good ideas. Leading-edge technology companies from 3M to Pixar to Google have made a science of optimizing the creativity of their employees, engineering working environments that encourage random interaction, collaboration, and even fun. That, in any case, is the design imperative behind the dramatic "space station" plan for Apple's proposed new $5 billion headquarters, the last initiative spearheaded by the late Steve Jobs.

Companies need not push the boundaries of architecture and interior design to embrace combinatorial innovation. It's just as easy to open your doors to outside developers and simply ask them to work on problems on your behalf, offering modest prizes or the pledge to work with them to develop fully the most promising experiments they can hack together in an artificially short period of time.

That's the theory, in any case, behind the growing trend toward hackathons—largely informal events where enterprises invite developers to compete in timed projects to develop new solutions to persistent market problems. At first a Silicon Valley innovation, hackathons have spread around the world.

Leveraging a growing cottage industry of freelance developers and do-it-yourselfers, hackathons are easy to organize and can generate impressive results. The Web site TechCrunch, among many others, runs regular hackathon events around the country, judged by tech-savvy celebrities such as Ashton Kutcher and leading venture investors. A recent TechCrunch Disrupt event in New York attracted two thousand participants. The annual Consumer Electronics Show in Las Vegas includes dozens of hackathons, some spontaneously generated.

To improve our own access to early market experiments, we often serve as hackathon judges. An inspiring 2013 event we attended was sponsored by AT&T and Ericsson and held at San Francisco–based Hattery, a fast-growing technology incubator founded by former Google executives. AT&T provided the space, code samples, and ample carbohydrates. Seasoned developers and other "sensei" roamed the room, helping teams organize, focus their idea, and develop working prototypes.

The goal of the hackathon was to develop smartphone applications that would help children and adults suffering from autism, as well as their families. Teams included everyone from autism activists to seasoned technology executives to high school students, who worked until late on a Friday night, and then all day Saturday. The apps they presented did everything from customizing flash cards for improved name recognition to simulating difficult social interactions and providing gentle feedback.

In the end, more than twenty teams demoed their apps, many of which appeared close to completion. The winning team, whose members didn't all know each other at the beginning of the event, split a $10,000 prize. Perhaps more important, they gained valuable exposure to leaders in the powerful mobile ecosystem that continues to spawn Big Bang Disruptors at an accelerating pace.

Once hackathons end, however, there's no reason the continued development of market experiments need revert to old-fashioned command-and-control research. Following what's called the "lean start-up" model, full development and even product launch can continue without the organizational overhead of a formal business. Discontinuous drops in transaction costs have made it much easier for developers with no manufacturing, distribution, or internal IT capacity to find producers for their goods on the global market. The economics of Big Bang Disruption have effectively shrunk the optimal size of the start-up firm to just a few individuals.

For incumbents hoping to play an active role in the Singularity, embracing direct-market experimentation may require a significant cultural shift. When disruptive technologies began life neither better nor cheaper, companies that wanted to introduce them in next-generation products needed ways of funding expensive experiments. This often meant selling higher-priced products with limited capabilities to niche markets and customers that needed the technology badly enough to serve as willing test subjects, paying more for less.

With both the experience and the funding supplied by these customers, innovators could continue developing the disruptor until it reached mainstream price and performance, at which point the innovator could leverage both its market and technical expertise to "cross the chasm" to mass market customers.

With better and cheaper disruptors enabled by exponential technologies, however, that approach may prove not only unnecessary but also counterproductive. In the Singularity, the infrastructure is in place for direct-market experimentations. Incumbents must learn the ways of the lean start-up, combining available parts into working products just to see who buys them and what they do with them. With new forms of collaboration, new tools, and falling costs for testing experiments directly in the market, the value of combine is rapidly outpacing the value of design.

In the early days of what many expect to be a massive future market for 3-D printing, the old and new approaches to disruption are being tested against each other.

3D Systems, which began life producing industrial-grade prototyping machines for manufacturers of prosthetic limbs, helicopters, and medical devices, moved into mass market printers following the traditional model. By starting with custom solutions built for premium customers, 3D Systems developed valuable expertise, goodwill, and financial capital.

As the cost of 3-D technology continued to decline, the company carefully timed its entry into the consumer market, offering its first home 3-D printer, the Cube, in early 2012. The Cube produces objects around six inches square, and sold for $1,299 when first announced. The company's industrial-strength printers, by comparison, cost anywhere from $10,000 to $100,000.

3D Systems's approach contrasts sharply with start-up competitor MakerBot, which launched its first product with little in the way of prior experience, either as a maker of 3-D printers or of anything else. The company was founded by a former school teacher and some industrial experimenters he met at a Brooklyn hackathon. Their goal was and remains to give individuals the tools to create and share their own personal innovations, whether artistic or practical.

From years of close association with Maker Faire attendees, MakerBot's founders recognized that the component parts for cheap 3-D printing were already available in 2009. 3-D printers, in fact, were already being cobbled together by individual hobbyists, who shared their design and expertise freely and enthusiastically. MakerBot offered its first consumer product that year, and has since sold more than twenty-two thousand printers.

MakerBot's competitive strengths go beyond early entry. The company's real energy goes into nurturing its Thingiverse, a free platform where users share their designs and expertise with other users. To support that community, the company has emphasized the use of standard parts and open-source specifications in its devices.

In 2013, MakerBot was acquired by Stratasys Ltd., 3D System's biggest traditional competitor, in a deal that valued MakerBot's DIY culture at over $600 million. Stratasys, like 3D Systems, has technological and applications expertise. But MakerBot is much closer to the user community. In buying the start-up, Stratasys appears to be hedging its bets in entering the consumer market.

If the merged entity can find synergy in two very different corporate cultures, it will be a victory for unencumbered development over 3D Systems's strengths in high-end technical and business expertise. To succeed, 3D Systems, like other incumbents, must continue to maintain a delicate balance between leveraging its business-to-business experience without overly identifying with the needs of current customers.

In the Singularity, incumbent innovators who once profited from building to customer specification often find their traditional advantages turn into disadvantages. Within the condensed life cycle of Big

Bang Disruption, there's no time to focus on different market segments, moving carefully from high-end to mass market. Disruptors must start out building to the market—or, better, giving the market the tools to do the building itself.

As the example of MakerBot suggests, lean start-ups don't just engage new kinds of participants in their early market experiments. They also make use of different raw materials, including off-the-shelf hardware components and reusable software, designs, and even business infrastructure. And they experiment in plain sight of customers and competitors. That's because the benefits of engaging early users in market experiments outweigh the value of surprising competitors with a finished product. Developing new products and services in "stealth mode" is a thing of the past.

That's the lesson of a start-up called Oculus VR, which is creating low-cost 3-D head-mounted displays for immersive new video games, and doing so in full view of users and competitors alike. Perhaps that's because its founder, Palmer Luckey, didn't know any other way. Until recently, Luckey was not an entrepreneur but rather a community college student.

He was also a fanatical gamer, one dissatisfied with current display products. Luckey obsessively bought outdated military and other industry-specific virtual-reality equipment off of eBay, hoping to find something that would work for video games. He soon realized that the custom and often expensive features of specialized displays made them worse, rather than better, for video games. So Luckey hacked together his own solution using cannibalized parts, including two cell-phone screens and a pair of ski goggles. The Oculus Rift was born.

With enthusiastic encouragement from game industry veterans, Luckey and a few partners launched a Kickstarter campaign that raised nearly $2.5 million in its first month. While many of the obsolete products Luckey started with originally sold for thousands of dollars, Oculus VR's developer kit costs only $300. With prelaunch buzz running high, a consumer product is set to release soon.

In hardware, general-purpose computer processors, sensors, displays, and user-interface devices can be cobbled into new devices with little customization. For software-enabled services and apps, advances in software engineering over the last two decades have made it even easier to reuse code. Common functions are increasingly being embedded in operating systems and other middleware. Even specialized algorithms for creating machine-readable bar codes or for speech recognition are being offered as open source or licensed at minimal costs.

With the rise of big data, proprietary data warehouses are likewise evolving rapidly into recombinable products available for experimentation. Vast cloud-based databases, such as Google's geographic data and the European Union's Open Data project, organized in standard formats and published interfaces, are offered for free or by license.

The network effects generated by sharing this data explains why research costs are falling not just in business but even in science, in fields as distant from software as materials and basic chemistry. According to the National Human Genome Research Institute, for example, the cost per raw megabase of DNA sequences fell from $10,000 in 2001 to just ten cents in 2013, while the cost per sequenced human genome dropped in the same period from $100 million to a few thousand. As open-source software, standardized databases, and cloud-based storage and processing are embraced by researchers in every field, the momentum toward unencumbered development is accelerating.

That's largely because digital "parts," including software and data, don't get used up, lowering, if not eliminating, the cost of basic materials. "Now what we see," says Google chief economist Hal Varian, "is a period where you have Internet components, where you have software, protocols, languages, and capabilities to combine these component parts in ways that create totally new innovations." As Varian explains:

> You can reproduce them, you can duplicate them, you can spread them around the world, and you can have thousands and tens of thousands of innovators combining or recombining the same component parts to create new innovation. So there's no shortage. There are no inventory delays. It's a situation where the components are available for everyone, and so we get this tremendous burst of innovation that we're seeing.

These examples reveal more than just the increasing advantage of combinatorial innovation. They also reflect a new approach to basic research in general. Rather than take on an industry's biggest problems head-on with bold, expensive R&D, Big Bang Disruption starts with narrow experiments in markets for new products, often intentionally limited to short production runs as with NeoLucida. Limited trials can be great test beds, generating revenue, experience, and reusable and recombinable data sources.

Innovators and their investors take what they learn from these experiments and rapidly apply them in adjacent markets. In industries such as health care and public utilities, where regulatory barriers to entry have desensitized incumbents to the threat of new entrants, entrepreneurs can often experiment in plain sight without being noticed. This allows for rapid innovation at the margins of an industry's major technological obstacles. Just as important, it puts off potentially deadly political and legal fights until the disruptor is ready for its big reveal.

Right now, for example, innovators are performing early market experiments in new forms of disposable chemical batteries and other sources of low-cost power generation. Launched in 2013, the portable recharger PowerTrekk utilizes basic principles of experimental hydrogen fuel cells to create emergency charging batteries for mobile electronics. Scoop up some water, and a disposable cartridge filled with basic chemicals extracts the hydrogen to charge a small battery, leaving sand as the residual product.

In the energy sector, the development of high-end hydrogen fuel cells has been going on for years, focused on electricity generation and rechargeable cells for vehicles. Development costs are high, progress has been slow, and environmental concerns are hard to define or alleviate. PowerTrekk offers the same basic technology, but on such a small scale that it can use simpler chemistry and inert materials.

That approach has not only led to a commercial product, but may ultimately point to solutions for the industry's most intractable problems. It is precisely the kind of unencumbered development that incumbent energy companies should be watching closely, if not performing themselves.

Large-scale disruption in energy and other regulated industries, however, may just as easily emerge from the edges of the industry as from its core. That's because the scale of such industries is so immense that even small improvements in efficiency and price can shift the balance of power and profits. Given the legal constraints on regulated incumbents, better and cheaper performance may originate with unregulated outsiders exploiting new data sources, networks, and devices to introduce information services that separate providers from their customers. Without solving any of the industry's fundamental problems, these new tools can still generate significant efficiency improvements while building expertise that can spawn future disruptors.

In the electricity industry, for example, substantial efficiencies are being realized as part of the development of what are called "smart grids." In a smart grid, power plants, distribution networks, meters, and even individual sockets collect usage and demand information in real time using a variety of sensors and other component technologies. Analysis and reporting of that information can stimulate more efficient behaviors, including load balancing by power generators and less wasteful consumption by businesses and home users.

Information collected by smart grids promise more dynamic pricing, better integration of nonrenewable and renewable energy sources, reduced power theft, and improved design for everything from power plants down to the devices that rely on them. Estimates put the potential savings from better information tools and interfaces as high as one hundred billion dollars over the next twenty years. By 2014, the market for smart energy products worldwide is projected to grow to nearly $200 billion.

While generators, distributors, and other traditional industry participants are likely to be leading participants and beneficiaries of smart-grid technology, the scope of the savings has already proven irresistible to entrepreneurs and their investors. In the past few years, dozens of venture-backed start-ups have been launched to capitalize on the opportunity, including companies developing monitoring software for smart homes and buildings and designing the advanced sensors for deployment all along the existing power grid. Seemingly random experimentation, much of it based on combinatorial innovations, is in full swing.

There is, however, one potent counterweight to the creative and economic liberation afforded by combinatorial innovation: the global patent system. Patents, which grant short-term monopolies for innovators to make or license their inventions, assume a model dominated by design rather than combine. As with copyright, legal protection for inventions, which were developed as part of the industrial revolution, has been optimized for products with high development, manufacturing, and distribution costs.

The goal of patent protection is to stimulate the production of disruptive innovations, but today many inventors believe that protection is doing more harm than good. As national legislatures and patent offices worldwide have struggled to adapt the patent system to combinable innovations such as software, there is little doubt that the current patent system is in crisis.

Even the world's largest companies are looking for solutions to the patent morass. Some are forming patent pools, where competitors throw all their patents together and agree, in exchange for freedom from expensive and time-consuming litigation, to cross-license the entire bundle at reasonable rates to all comers.

As governments look for solutions to the patent problem, there are still ways for incumbents to leverage their intellectual property as a kind of currency in collaborations with entrepreneurs in the Singularity.

Industrial giant GE, for one, has taken the lead in finding creative ways to balance patent protection with the power of unencumbered development. The company recently partnered with Quirky, a virtual network for inventors that helps turn ideas into market experiments and, eventually, successful products.

GE agreed to license thousands of its patents to Quirky members in hopes of accelerating the development of technologies to support the Internet of Things—a key area of potential products and services for the largest and most profitable infrastructure company in the world. GE will share in the revenue of any successful products developed with its patents, trading its intellectual property for access to the creative energy of Quirky's 360,000 registered users—denizens of the Singularity.

"There are a host of consumer applications that we haven't had the ability to focus on," GE's chief marketing officer said of the partnership with Quirky in a *New York Times* interview. "That just isn't our core business."

Yet the company's "core business" is—and always has been—the creation of new products and services that create new markets, new industries, and phenomenal new value for the company. Which is to say, markets built on Big Bang Disruption. For GE and other disruptive innovators, in other words, it isn't the mission that's changed. Just the tools.

The new tools, at the same time, might be simple—simple enough to describe in barely a sentence. As we'll see in the next stage.

CHAPTER 5
THE BIG BANG
SURVIVING CATASTROPHIC SUCCESS

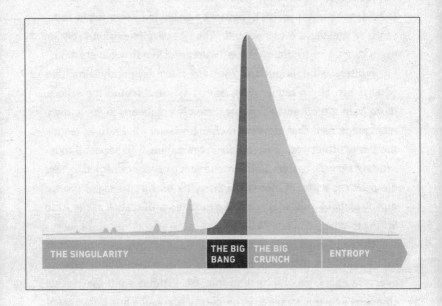

THE SINGULARITY | THE BIG BANG | THE BIG CRUNCH | ENTROPY

witter only looks simple. The microblogging service appears to be little more than a multiuser text messaging service, distributing users' 140-character "tweets" to groups of their followers, allowing them in turn to follow other users. Users can also retweet comments they like, and search globally for comments by topic. To outsiders, the service is just an enhancement to SMS messaging, which has been around for decades.

Yet Twitter's unprecedented growth from a handful of internal users in 2006 to two hundred million in 2013 suggests something revolutionary has happened. Nearly half a billion tweets flow through the system every day. Celebrity entertainers, athletes, and politicians such as Lady Gaga, Cristiano Ronaldo, and Barack Obama have tens of millions of followers.

During popular events that range from Beyoncé's pregnancy to the final moments of the European soccer championships to more serious subjects, including the earthquake and tsunami that devastated Japan's coast in 2011, Twitter's worldwide users tweet thousands of messages every second. Almost every television program urges its viewers to "follow us on Twitter and join the conversation."

Twitter's straightforward user interface brilliantly simplifies what is actually a highly complicated system. Behind the scenes, more than a thousand employees, mostly engineers, juggle a technical juggernaut that grows and changes faster all the time, testing the limits of network design and optimization. The service's thousands of servers, routers, and switches have been architected to handle peak capacities of more than thirty thousand tweets per second during global events that can spike the site's traffic, such as the Arab Spring that began in late 2010.

The company's basic innovation of transforming short messages into a real-time, global social network has resonated with users in every category, geography, and interest. Estimates put the private company's current value, as its owners prepare for a first public offering, at $10 billion.

Yet in the crucial early years of its existence, Twitter, like many Big Bang Disruptors, was nearly undone by sudden popularity. When users took to the service beyond the wildest dreams of its founders, the company lacked the infrastructure or the personnel needed to deliver a stable, commercial version of the product.

Indeed, at the time of Twitter's public launch in 2007, it's fair to say that the service was more experiment than commercial product. There was little of what one might call a business, let alone one prepared to become one of the most recognized brands in the world.

The most serious problems were technical. Twitter's original design proved difficult to scale. Despite heroic efforts, well into 2008 the service regularly experienced ten or more hours of unavailability every month. During its frequent outages, Twitter's highly addictive scrolling feed of tweets was replaced by the static image of a serene whale being lifted delicately out of the water by tiny birds. The "fail whale" became so familiar to frustrated users that they hardly needed the accompanying message, "Twitter is over capacity."

Management "fails" exacerbated the engineering mishaps. The company had been founded by three young entrepreneurs, one of them still an undergraduate at the time, who had little experience or interest in building a global business. Frustrated by repeated handoffs of the senior executive job among the founders, investors pushed for more seasoned leadership.

Finally, in 2010, the company announced it was promoting chief operating officer Dick Costolo to the job of CEO. Costolo, who had joined the company a year earlier, was a former Google executive with extensive experience bringing start-ups from experiment to fully functioning enterprises.

The company now stands on more stable technical and business ground, with Costolo pushing for partnerships and other forms of revenue for the start-up. The company has expanded its program of "sponsored tweets" and recently announced plans to host video-clip highlights from broadcasters.

Twitter suffered—and survived—what we call "catastrophic success," one of the most visible characteristics of the second stage of the shark fin—the Big Bang.

Big Bang Disruption devastates existing markets in two ways—gradually and then suddenly. The Singularity, the wild period of failed early market experiments, produces gradual disruption. In the Big Bang, everything is sudden, including success and failure. Customers either arrive at once or not at all. Instead of slow, controlled progress through discrete market segments, Big Bang Disruptors have only two main categories of customers—trial users and everybody else. Where Chapter Four focused on test runs aimed at trial users, here we look at the other segment: everybody else.

Big Bang markets are by their nature "winner take all." In this stage of the shark fin, time seems to move at an accelerated pace—for entrepreneurs, their customers, and most of all for incumbents who wake up one morning to find their core products and technologies displaced by something better and cheaper. A lead of just a few months or even few weeks can make the difference between unparalleled victory and ignoble defeat.

Because Big Bang Disruptors experience unconstrained growth driven by near-perfect market information, new products and services spread virally. Customers drive extreme market demand even as they continually rewrite the business case on behalf of the disrupter. Innovators, whether start-up or incumbent, must learn to see the signs of imminent success, and learn to survive the rapid acceleration that accompanies it.

To survive the Big Bang, you'll need the business equivalent of a time machine. How do you measure changing market conditions quickly enough to satisfy unprecedented demand when it suddenly arrives? What can you do to come out the victor in new winner-take-all markets? If your next disruption isn't yet ready, what can you do to slow the progress of others?

In this chapter, we answer these questions with examples of Big Bang Disruptors whose creators managed or in some cases failed to follow the next three rules in this brief but crucial stage:

Rule 4. *Survive Catastrophic Success*—Prepare to scale up from experiment to global brand in the space of months, if not weeks, and to redesign your technical and business architecture even while running at full speed. Watch for emerging standards that signal the maturing of winning technologies

Rule 5. *Capture Winner-Take-All Markets*—Sacrifice everything, including short-term profits, to ensure victory in winner-take-all markets, especially when success with one disruptor can be leveraged into follow-on products that can be created and launched even faster than the original.

Rule 6. *Create Bullet Time*—Judiciously employ litigation and legislation to slow the progress of disruptors, even as you proceed with your own experiments, partnerships, and well-timed acquisitions.

RULE 4. SURVIVE CATASTROPHIC SUCCESS

Thanks to the low cost of experimentation and the availability of robust platforms for delivery and direct market feedback, the transition from Singularity to Big Bang happens quickly, even suddenly. When the right combination of technologies and business model comes together, the market is primed for sudden adoption. Consumers have already seen and experienced the failures. They know both what they want and what it looks like.

The catastrophic success of Big Bang Disruptors is the natural consequence of near-perfect market information. Rather than sellers broadcasting select information to potential customers, consumers pull information from other consumers on price, quality, and customer service, whenever and wherever they are. Advertising is both customized and timely, and often comes in the form of trusted referrals.

The availability of near-perfect market information also means consumers make fewer mistakes. They don't buy something that might be good enough simply because manufacturers invest in more advertising. They wait until the right version—3-D televisions, electric cars, solar power—emerges. Almost-there versions don't sell poorly; they don't sell at all.

Incumbents trained to develop marketing plans based on the bell curve model of technology adoption will need to make serious adjustments. The best marketing is provided ad hoc by early users, increasing in value thanks to network effects. Instead of planning marketing campaigns, companies must learn to leverage the power of their customers' information networks.

To survive catastrophic success, innovators must anticipate the moment when failed early market experiments are ready to make the leap to Big Bang Disruptors. Missing the moment means missing the market.

The history of technological innovation is littered with potential disruptors that may have offered superior price, performance, and quality but failed to create needed momentum at the moment users were ready to adopt a winner. That list includes Sony's Betacam, which lost out to JVC's more freely licensed VHS format, as well as Blu-Ray's victory over HD-DVD decades later. In these and other examples, the winners might not have had better technology. They were just in the right place at the right time, ready to scale when the market matured.

Going back to the 1890s, the early days of the automobile featured a technology standards war of its own, with steam-, electric-, and gasoline-powered vehicles vying for Big Bang status. As cars became affordable for mainstream consumers, steam clearly had the upper hand, with the Stanley Steamer setting the world speed record of 122 miles per hour in 1909.

The company erred, however, in pricing its car as a luxury item. Then, adoption stalled at a critical moment when public horse troughs—which its cars used to refuel—were briefly closed in 1914 following an outbreak of hoof-and-mouth disease. Electric cars, meanwhile, were held back by the limited driving range of early batteries.

Gasoline cars succeeded largely by avoiding such strategic errors and technical obstacles. As adoption accelerated, they were able to cut production costs and mitigate the high up-front investment needed to support a network of gasoline stations. Adoption accelerated, sealing the fate of alternative technologies. Once the industry achieved momentum, gasoline-powered cars were hard to stop.

Knowing the right moment and being ready for it has become more urgent in the world of exponential technologies. Consider Dollar Shave Club, a subscription razor-blade service launched in 2012. Dollar Shave Club found itself the victim of catastrophic success when its clever YouTube commercial went viral, quickly logging ten million views. Traffic to the company's Web site spiked, exceeding the hosting service's ability to keep up.

The company scrambled to fill some twelve thousand orders that arrived just in the first forty-eight hours. "It was terrifying," Dollar Shave Club founder Michael Dubin told the *New York Times*. "After working for a year and half and making all the sacrifices to get to this point, you realize your greatest dream is turning into your biggest nightmare. Maybe we're going to blow our big moment."

Surviving catastrophic success, as Dubin learned, requires fearless, even arrogant and potentially dangerous, planning. As innovators launch their experiments, they must be prepared for outrageous, sudden success. That means having in place the inventory, systems, and human resources necessary to fill orders, service the needs of a new and potentially large customer base, and start working on follow-up products and new versions of the original disruptor.

Many Big Bang Disruptors fail to reach their potential simply because their developers plan for normal growth and can't adjust fast enough when market adoption becomes vertical. Hedging a new product launch increasingly means planning for failure.

But what if adoption stalls before you expect it to? Getting caught with resources you didn't need after all, assuming you could afford them in the first place, is likely a fatal error. Any Silicon Valley investor can tell you horror stories of start-ups that hired too fast, built too far ahead of capacity, or that transitioned from a few entrepreneurs to a fully staffed enterprise before the true disruptive product had been engineered.

The result is nearly always the same: the investment fails and the company disappears. Finding what little salvage value may remain—usually in patents and other intellectual property—is the special domain of what are known as "vulture capitalists."

The best solution is to line up third-party resources and arrange to outsource as much of the scaling needs as possible on short—perhaps very short—notice. The winning balance requires experimenters who strike it big to rely as much as possible on virtual supply chains, where capacity can be added and subtracted without having to retool the experiment. That includes cloud-based services for information, and flexible manufacturing techniques for physical components.

Doing so may be relatively easy for software products and information services that are entirely digital, where scalable infrastructure is available on demand from providers around the world. Storage, Web site hosting, order processing, and communications can all be rapidly increased or decreased behind the scenes.

For physical goods, the problem is not so easily avoided. When colleagues directed us to glowing reviews of a new line of Ultrabooks, we visited the manufacturer's site to order one. After going through the company's do-it-yourself configuration tool, which cleverly outsources most presales service directly to the customer, we were told that the entire line was backordered for at least ninety days. No firm delivery date was available. We were welcome to pay in full to save a place in a waiting line of unknown length. We declined.

Clearly, we weren't the only customers who had seen the reviews. Unfortunately for the manufacturer, the life span for a "hit" computing device these days is well under ninety days, and by the time the model was again available, the market had moved on. The company had successfully sold its available inventory at launch, but left an unknown amount of revenue on the table by failing to plan for dramatic success.

It also left a bad taste in the mouths of disappointed potential customers, who may be less likely to buy from the company in the future—and likely to share that fact with their social networks.

To its credit—and likely its survival—room-sharing start-up Airbnb recognized its own scaling crisis in time. When the volume of e-mails from customers and hosts suddenly jumped from a few dozen a day to over a thousand in 2011, the service's Aircorps, as its customer service staff are known, began falling behind. Response times went from a few hours to a few days. That's when volume began to fall, a potentially catastrophic event for a company trying to establish its service as a Big Bang Disruptor.

The company's leaders recognized a make-or-break moment for the start-up, and radically altered their approach to human resources. After four months of nonstop hiring and training boot camps, Airbnb managed to triple the size of its Aircorps. As a result, for the first time since the service was launched, customer service capacity began to exceed the volume of service requests, a gap that has since widened. Management has committed to maintaining that shift now that the service has returned to steady growth.

As these examples underscore, near-perfect market information means that the success of new products and services is increasingly determined by the quality of customer service—a big gap for many companies. Review sites where real customers give frank assessments not just of product quality but pre- and post-sales support can sink even the best product—and consumers often start their research by reading the worst reviews.

Learning to leverage existing users as customer-support partners can be the key to surviving catastrophic success. Early users often feel a sense of ownership for products they experimented with first, and are more than happy to volunteer on "ask me anything" community message boards.

That's an especially valuable asset for start-up organizations without the capacity or experience to serve mainstream markets. For incumbents with existing customer service departments, outsourcing to early users means not only tolerating but encouraging a substantial loss of control—a difficult but crucial shift.

Surviving catastrophic success also requires as much warning as possible—knowing not only which of your new products and services consumers will embrace, but when. You need tools to help pinpoint the moment early market experiments are ready to shift to sudden adoption.

We have cataloged several early warning signs of imminent take-off. Perhaps most telling, according to our research, is the rise of competing standards for new technologies. Standards simplify the process of combinatorial innovation, making it easier to mix and match components. And developer alliances formed to promote competing alternatives provide a road map for the ecosystem that is emerging to implement them.

When innovators are simply playing with new capabilities, there's little need for a robust ecosystem of suppliers, distributors, and retailers to deliver and extend potential disruptors. As exponential technologies make the leap to the Big Bang stage, however, common interfaces, data exchanges, and network architectures are essential to support mass adoption.

A standards battle is heating up, for example in the Internet of

Things (IoT), reflecting the rapid expansion of the early market experiments we described in Chapter Two. In experiments to expand connectivity to devices of all shapes and sizes, innovators have already employed several incompatible communications protocols, frequencies, and networks. Unfortunately, that means there's no guarantee that any given device will be able to communicate with the others, or that the volumes of data being sent and received will be coherent to application developers trying to analyze them.

As more devices become intelligent and more data are being captured and put to use, there are now several competing standards vying for developer, supplier, and consumer adoption. Some are being promoted on the open-source model, while others are proprietary.

An alliance of developers, regulators, and incumbent consumer electronics manufacturers have aligned behind ZigBee, for example. ZigBee works on a low-power network that operates in unlicensed ranges of radio spectrum, cleverly increasing the distance data can travel by taking advantage of intermediary devices to relay information through compliant networks.

Broadcom, which produces IoT chips that can be embedded directly into consumer goods, however, has rejected ZigBee and other specific standards in favor of generic communications protocols such as WiFi and Bluetooth, the approach taken as well by Belkin for its WeMo product.

While the generic solutions require more power and operate over shorter distances, they have the advantage of momentum—most consumers already have WiFi routers in their homes, making it easy to piggyback off an infrastructure that is already familiar and in place.

As in most standards battles, technical superiority is only one factor in determining a winner. A dominant IoT standard is far from clear, in any case. Industry insiders believe the war will be won, as it often is, by the solution that best simplifies consumer adoption—that is, the one that most quickly exhibits the kind of network effects we described in Chapter Two.

Standards fights are also frequent in industries that historically suffer from high transaction costs, characterized by markets with many sellers having little market influence, or industries dominated by nonprofit participants, regulatory constraints, or both. These institutional limits can operate as barriers to disruption, sometimes unintentionally, and often for long periods.

In such industries, which include such disparate examples as higher education and financial payment processing, the potential for exponential technologies to deliver Big Bang Disruption may be apparent long before market experiments make the leap to true disruptor. Consumers may already be ready, willing, and able to participate in a more efficient ecosystem. The problem may be that the industry just can't get itself moving.

The push to adopt a technical standard in such cases is often just a symptom of stalled efforts to overcome intractable inefficiencies in the supply chain. Standardization, in other words, may be necessary simply to force long-overdue consolidation, reorganization, and simplification in the industry in general.

Consider education. Since much of the industry operates as nonprofit enterprises, the incentives to adopt technologies that discontinuously reduce transaction costs are rarely market-driven. Students have little bargaining leverage, and administrators have limited authority to expand the institution virtually using the Internet and mobile technologies—even those, including video streaming and digital content, that are both mature and firmly established in other ecosystems. Faculty members are caught in the middle, torn between their loyalty to the schools at which they hold tenure and the opportunity to reach a wider audience with their expertise.

Pressure (some of it political, in the case of budget-strapped public universities) has been building for years. Now technology is forcing the issue. Early market experiments in massive open online courses (or MOOCs) have proven wildly popular, attracting millions of participants. By 2011, over 30 percent of all students enrolled in degree programs had taken at least one online course.

The willingness of virtual students to embrace distance learning has spawned a hotbed of experimentation from private-sector outsiders, including the nonprofit Kahn Academy and the venture-funded Udemy. Their MOOC platforms compete with those being offered by different coalitions of research universities, including edX, Udacity, and Coursera.

Still, whether as providers or suppliers, the universities remain tentative, worried that widespread adoption could diminish their brand and the value of limited enrollments in residential programs. In some cases, the new standards are simply too radical for incumbents to handle. Kahn Academy, founded by former hedge fund manager Salman Kahn, rejects the classroom paradigm altogether, promoting instead an interactive problem-driven learning model. By 2013, Kahn Academy was reaching six million unique users each month.

While education suppliers continue to debate the nature of their mission in the face of new technologies for learning, the winning standard seems likely, again, to be driven by consumers, who are unburdened by the philosophical angst of the incumbent providers. MOOC users just want the personal and financial benefits of higher education, and are eager to take advantage of available technology to reduce the costs, inconvenience, and other overhead of the existing university supply chain, which has evolved little since the Middle Ages.

Structural obstacles have also long stood in the way of more efficient payment-processing technologies. As the financial services industry moves slowly but inevitably from a combination of cash, paper checks, and credit/debit cards to one dominated by secure mobile payments using smartphones and other devices, banks, credit card processors, and financial services corporations have engaged in only tepid experimentation. They fear losing control—and with it the predicable profitability—of the current systems, however inefficient they may be.

At the same time, legal restrictions on banking, financial information, and consumer credit make it difficult for technology-driven start-ups, including Google Wallet, PayPal, Square, and Isis, to aggressively disrupt an increasingly fragile payment processing supply chain. Several competing technologies (QR codes, SMS payments), standards (Trusted Execution Environment, Near Field Communications), and platforms (LevelUp, Paydiant, and the retailer-based MCX), deployed by competing alliances of old and new industry participants, are vying to find the Big Bang Disruptor.

In both education and payment processing, the adoption of standards are slowed or even stalled by aging regulatory systems. Legal counterweights loom large in both industries. To be competitive, start-up online educational institutions need accreditation—credentials that governments may withhold in order to protect the universities and colleges they already fund and often operate. Payment processors must likewise partner with existing supply-chain participants to avoid running afoul of extensive banking and consumer credit laws.

The $4.4 trillion education market and the $171 billion spent globally on payment processing are prizes too rich to hold off devastating innovation much longer. Market pressure from customers, frustrated by the inefficiency and cost of existing options, is also building. A few experiments will surely succeed and, driven ahead by near-perfect market information, quickly dominate. When they do, those involved—start-up and incumbent alike—will need to be prepared for catastrophic success.

RULE 5. CAPTURE WINNER-TAKE-ALL MARKETS

For those who survive catastrophic success, the payoff can be enormous. Big Bang Disruptors frequently dominate the new categories and new markets they create even after saturation is reached. Success often translates to winner-take-all markets, where even fast followers must settle for a small fraction of the disrupter's market share and, often, a much lower price for similar goods.

A tendency toward winner-take-all markets is the natural result of removing artificial barriers to competition such as tariffs and other trade restrictions and allowing global markets to evolve on their own terms. For commodity goods and services, by definition, the lowest priced offering is the one every rational buyer would prefer. As a result, markets for goods with high transportation costs have historically been dominated by local participants, who can transport to local buyers at the lowest price.

Even leaving transportation aside, high transaction costs have made it difficult for buyers and sellers to find each other and share information to reach optimal arrangements. With the availability of near-perfect market information, however, those costs are being discontinuously reduced, disrupting local markets and undermining the complex supply chains of intermediary agents, distributors, and retailers. Consumers band together through the global Internet to advise one another on every conceivable aspect of products and services—including features, price, availability, service level, and quality.

There's nothing new, of course, about buyers and sellers sharing information about their dealings with each other. Graffiti found scrawled in the ruins of Pompeii includes enthusiastic reviews of the services of attendants in its Roman baths. Professional critics have spiced up the pages of newspapers and magazines for hundreds of years, and companies including Zagat (acquired by Google in 2011), Michelin, Consumer Reports, and Angie's List together earn billions of dollars as tastemakers in specialized categories including high-end restaurants, consumer products, and local service providers.

Not-for-profits, including the Better Business Bureau, the Chamber of Commerce, and licensing and professional associations of service providers from plumbers to financial advisers, allow industries to set and enforce their own quality standards to help consumers efficiently separate professionals from amateurs. Trademarks, in fact, originated with the fiercely enforced standards of local medieval guilds—another shortcut to help buyers choose wisely.

Today, there are dedicated review services for everything from music and other entertainment to the sustainability practices of global multinationals. Everyone has an opinion, in many cases several of them. Discovering commentary and feedback that is the most reliable and most in sync with our own preferences gets easier all the time, a feature of the larger disruptive power of big data.

The concentration of winner-take-all markets in Big Bang Disruption, however, is driven by the sudden convergence of a remarkable supply of information into resources and tools that can be easily and automatically searched, sorted, and compared, often at the point of transaction decision making. Consumers across traditional marketing categories, demographics, and geographies increasingly work together as a unit, implicitly expressing their collective preferences with ruthless efficiency.

Beyond dedicated review sites and simple Web searches, artificial intelligence is being employed to develop search engines that learn. Recommendations based on transaction history, and coordination with preferences of similar users, can produce powerful results. Amazon, a leader here, has continuously tweaked its algorithms to deliver more insight in its recommendations on every category it sells by itself or through its partners.

Likewise, entertainment distributor Netflix can predict what movies a user is likely to want to watch. The company has begun using its vast database of customer preferences to design original content, including its first produced miniseries, a remake of the BBC's *House of Cards*, which cost the company a reported $100 million to create. Netflix's analysis revealed that viewers of the original series also liked director David Fincher and actor Kevin Spacey, who were already attached to the project.

As a company spokesman told *Wired* magazine in 2012, "We know what people watch on Netflix and we're able with a high degree of confidence to understand how big a likely audience is for a given show based on people's viewing habits." Though the company has refused to release viewing data, estimates based on ISP traffic suggest that each episode of *House of Cards* has been streamed by between 1.5 and 2.7 million viewers.

Internet radio stations, unlike their broadcast predecessors, can easily collect feedback about what its listeners want to hear and use that knowledge to improve their service. For Pandora, that information is paired with the specific features of each song or artist categorized by groups from Pandora's proprietary Music Genome Project to seed virtual "stations" that play songs with similar properties. User feedback refines the station's results, deemphasizing certain attributes when a user indicates she dislikes a particular song and emphasizing other attributes for those she prefers.

Understanding the mechanics of near-perfect market information, as these examples make clear, is essential for innovators competing in winner-take-all markets. There's no medal for second place and, more to the point, often very little market share or profit either. Even if competitors can attract customers, only the Big Bang Disruptor can command a price premium for its combination of largely commodity parts.

That premium reflects its status as a social and cultural meme—

think of the iPad tablet computer, Under Armour clothing, or Toyota's Prius. The gap in price between the Big Bang Disruptor and the also-rans can, in each of these categories, far outweigh any measurable difference in quality between them.

That lesson has become painfully clear in the intensely competitive market for flat-screen LCD televisions. While consumers may have once been willing to pay premium prices for the latest and greatest displays, advances in basic component technology have made it increasingly difficult for buyers to tell the difference between high-end brands and lower-price products that share many of the same parts from the same third-party sources. For now, Korean manufacturers, notably Samsung and LG, have largely taken over the market, sending longtime producers including Sharp, Sony, and Panasonic into steep decline.

As former leaders such as Sony and Panasonic are forced to cut production, the fall of Sharp has been especially devastating. Sharp's LCD sales fell 39 percent between 2008 and 2012. In 2012, the year the company celebrated its one hundredth anniversary, Sharp's share price dropped 70 percent in the first half of the year. The company's annual report that year ominously announced a "shift in categories"—moving from televisions to medical diagnostics, high-definition digital mirrors, and electronic textbooks.

As technologies both converge and improve rapidly, judging quality differences becomes difficult for consumers. As actual performance becomes commoditized, consumers move quickly to products rated the highest by other consumers while producers of only slightly lesser quality are forced to discount prices to attract enough customers to stay in business at all.

"In the past there was a huge gap between the best of breed and second best," an industry analyst explained to the *Washington Post*. "Now, maybe there's still a small gap between a Sony high-definition screen and an LG screen, but most consumers can't see it. And if most consumers can't see it, it's not there."

If second-place competitors struggle just to tread water in Big Bang markets, the prospects for weaker participants are even worse. In the heavyweight battle for smartphone dominance currently taking place between Apple and Samsung, for example, Nokia is falling farther behind. At its peak in 2003, Nokia sold more than 32 million mobile phones in North America, representing 20 percent of the company's global sales. But the company has been unable to translate its dominance into new markets for smartphones, selling fewer than 2.2 million in North America in 2012.

Pricing strategies can also help push a disruption from market experiment to true Big Bang Disruptor. Web-based companies have long been mocked for giving away new products and services with no clear plan to produce revenue, let alone profits. Yet in the face of winner-take-all markets, subsidizing or even giving away disruptive innovations for free can be a perfectly rational strategy.

Once the winner is established and its competitors relegated to the margins, disrupters can begin charging for premium versions, introduce advertising or other indirect sources of revenue, or extend their platform to adjacent products and services. Or they can simply start charging users who now have ample information to judge the product's true value.

This approach has become the norm for most smartphone and tablet apps, for example, and even for musicians or new authors establishing a base of fans for songs and e-books sold through Amazon, Apple, and other networks. In effect, the early adopter tax has become an early adopter rebate.

For disruptions that may be better but still not cheaper, sellers may find themselves compelled to subsidize early users. Tesla, the maker of luxury electric cars, is producing vehicles that, though certainly better on a number of dimensions, are by no means cheaper than other electric (let alone gas-fueled) luxury cars. Tesla's early strategy was to charge a premium price for the vehicles, an implied early adopter tax for customers who placed a high value on both luxury and environmental sustainability.

When that approach proved insufficient to generate projected sales volumes and market momentum, however, the company began to offer leasing plans for its premium vehicles, and to guarantee their resale value. Even then, the company's calculations of comparably valued luxury cars were immediately challenged by critics with access to near-perfect market information. A month later, Tesla had to adjust the plan, sweetening the guarantees.

Such seemingly irrational behavior may not only be essential to survive a winner-take-all market, it can pay dividends after early competitors have been vanquished. For one thing, the dominance that comes with winner-take-all markets allows the disruptor to construct its preferred revenue model in relative calm. Almost as important, being first past the post in the Big Bang stage can help the disruptor maintain its dominance through enhancements and extensions made possible by a large customer base.

The initial product may be improved, for example, by analyzing usage data that is a natural by-product of market dominance. Or the initial offering may serve as a platform on which other goods and services can be added, leveraging both the infrastructure and existing customers to cut both the cost and time needed to get to market. In that sense, winner-take-all markets can create virtuous circles, accelerating benefits to both producers and customers.

In the growing market for tax preparation services in the United States, three companies control over 90 percent of the market for self-prepared returns, a $2 billion business that covers nearly 40 percent of all returns filed. Of these, Intuit's TurboTax is the clear winner, with nearly 60 percent of the market. Acquired by Intuit in 1993, TurboTax takes advantage of its base of twenty-five million users to fine-tune its product, translating the most frequent customer service issues and tax questions into enhancements for next year's version.

The more people who use the product, the faster it improves—another example of network effects. Over the years, TurboTax has expanded from simple fill-in-the-blank software to an extensive online ecosystem, with hundreds of supporting videos and a network of tax professionals available to answer questions in real time. The product is also fully integrated with external data sources, and is able to populate returns with data from employers, brokerage firms, prior returns, and the company's personal financial software.

Or consider Apple's strategy for iTunes, which began life in 2001 as a legal alternative to early but unlicensed peer-to-peer music sharing experiments such as Napster. As users adapted to the idea of paid digital music, the iTunes store quickly became not only the leading digital music retailer, but the largest retailer of music in any medium. Ten years after launch, the service was available in 119 countries, pioneering a model of selling individual songs for a new market that wasn't constrained by the physical constraints of LPs and CDs. Revenue in 2012 topped $4 billion.

Music was only the first market to be reconfigured by the iTunes platform. With the technical infrastructure and user interface established, Apple extended its reach into the entertainment industry by adding movies, books, and television programming.

Having won the music market, Big Bang success elsewhere has come even more quickly. Apple's millions of users create powerful network effects, exerting strong gravitational pull on content providers to participate in the iTunes ecosystem. By mid-2013, the iTunes store had captured more than 65 percent of the market for digital movies and television programming—a market largely created by Apple.

RULE 6. CREATE BULLET TIME

The ability to move fast is critical in the Big Bang stage, whether for entrepreneurs or those whose businesses they disrupt. When a market experiment takes off, it's too late for long-term planning, much less the development of a competitive response. We've already seen the dangers of failing to plan for catastrophic success. The risk is high, but so is the reward—the potential for a winner-take-all market and the relative freedom to convert a single innovation into a platform for future disruptors.

What, if anything, can incumbents and other innovators do to slow down a runaway success before it comes up to full speed?

In *The Matrix* series of movies, comatose humans live in a dystopian future, plugged into a vast network of computers that use them as energy sources while the victims imagine themselves to be living real lives. The hero of the films, Neo, becomes aware of the delusion and develops the ability to manipulate the virtual environment against its digital overlords. In one famous scene, he uses that ability to slow the speed of bullets heading his way, giving him time to twist his body to avoid being shot.

Matrix producer Warner Bros. has trademarked this visual effect, known as "bullet time," where space and time become dramatically slowed and warped. In Big Bang Disruption, the technique is available to anyone. Applying it judiciously can often slow the pace of this short but crucial stage of transformation, buying you invaluable time to compete, partner, or simply acquire the disruptor before it devastates your business.

Slowing down the inevitable is especially important in regulated industries. While they often appear protected from Big Bang Disruption, the reality is that they are just as vulnerable, and in some respect even more at risk of devastation from information-driven disruptors.

Why? Because when the law implicitly or explicitly limits internal competition and bars new entrants, businesses have little, if any, incentive to innovate. As a result, regulated businesses—which include public utilities, air travel, defense, health care, and food and drugs—have fallen dangerously far behind in adopting exponential technologies. Once the disruptors do find a way in, collapse is that much more sudden.

Legal rules and regulations play another important role in the Big Bang stage. Our research reveals many examples of industry participants who earned valuable time to respond to disruptive innovations by deploying regulatory land mines to slow or even temporarily reverse the disruptors, overcoming the effects of near-perfect market information. They have proven themselves the most effective tool available to incumbents hoping to create bullet time.

We neither condone nor condemn the imposition of regulatory obstacles to slow the progress of Big Bang Disruption as it remakes existing industries. We want to emphasize, however, that bullet time, however achieved, is a temporary tool. As our research makes crystal clear, wherever there is exponential technology to exploit, Big Bang Disruption always happens . . . eventually. Bullet time may skew, slow, or even suspend innovation, but never for as long as incumbents hope it will.

We have already mentioned two of the most common techniques for achieving bullet time through regulation—the aggressive litigation of both patent and copyright claims by incumbents against start-ups and, in the case of patents, against other incumbents as well.

Patent litigation is by far the most effective creator of bullet time. By 2013, makers of smartphones were involved in more than one hundred patent disputes worldwide, with temporary injunctions creating a crazy quilt of restrictions on imports and exports in several countries. According to a widely reported Stanford University analysis, patent litigation and patent purchases cost smartphone makers up to $20 billion between 2011 and 2012; for the first time, patent-related spending by Apple and Google exceeded the companies' spending on research and development.

The use of patents as an offensive weapon has been unintentionally accelerated by overly generous grants for patents involving exponential technologies, including computer hardware and software. "The standards for granting patents are too loose," according to federal appellate judge Richard A. Posner, who, while sitting as a trial judge, dismissed one of the most notorious smartphone patent fights between Apple and Google. "There's a real chaos," Posner told the *New York Times*.

Still, chaos, no matter how achieved, translates to bullet time, even if, as in most patent wars, interrupted innovation is experienced by plaintiffs as well as defendants. Although systemic delays are a source of short-term advantage for litigants overwhelmed by the pace of disruptive technological change, they ultimately harm consumers, who must wait longer or pay more for better and cheaper new products that ought to be arriving at the speed of Moore's Law, not patent law.

Copyright, meanwhile, remains the preferred bullet time tool for entertainment companies, including producers of books, movies, and music. Having succeeded in shutting down the more brazen peer-to-peer file sharing services, content producers are spending heavily to block services that allow users to store large files in the cloud and have it available on any device they happen to be using.

Lawsuits against providers of so-called "digital locker" services maintain that some or perhaps much of the data users are storing are unlicensed copies of copyrighted content, and that the operators of such services should be held liable for the actions of their customers.

Music-sharing service Grooveshark, for example, which encourages users to upload music they lawfully purchased or even produced themselves, has fought a withering campaign against major record labels. "Part of the strategy of the major labels," the company's lawyer said in a 2012 interview, "is to burden start-ups that they view as threats with enormous legal fees to try to bring them to their knees." (Only two of the major labels have yet to license their content to the site—that is, to make it available on a legal basis.)

The labels complain that many of the music files uploaded by Grooveshark's users are unlicensed. The company counters that it does comply with copyright law by promptly removing unauthorized tracks and suspending offending consumers. Though the company has won small victories in its multiple ongoing lawsuits, the service has been barred from both Apple's and Google's app stores, cutting them off from the important mobile market. That and bad press from the litigation led to declining revenue and the loss of nearly half of Grooveshark's twenty-four million users. In late 2012 the company shed half its staff and consolidated its offices.

The company's hopes of survival look increasingly poor. Still, Grooveshark is only one of many digital distribution experiments in the volatile entertainment industry. So incumbents must continue to innovate, and at a faster pace, even as they litigate. They must offer legal versions of the services that consumers clearly want, and make those alternatives compelling for users. Otherwise, entertainment companies may well win all the legal battles but still lose the war.

In other industries, incumbents have learned to fight proxy wars, slowing the progress of Big Bang innovation by encouraging government agencies that oversee their own activities to gum up the engines of the disrupters. In the tightly controlled market for taxicab and limousine dispatching, for example, incumbents in cities around the world have used this tactic to slow or sometimes stop new virtual competitors, including Uber, SideCar, and Lyft.

The disruptors often construct their experiments carefully to avoid regulation, a technique we like to call "barely legal by design." Uber simply allows users to arrange for licensed limousines and, in some cities, taxicabs, using a smartphone app instead of a traditional dispatch service. Riders can track the location of their dispatched drivers using GPS, and pay directly on their phones. They can also rate the drivers. Uber doesn't provide its own vehicles or operators, but works with licensed drivers to help keep already-rolling vehicles busy transporting willing customers.

Legitimate health and safety concerns are valid reasons to oversee and even restrict the introduction of technology-based disruptors. But such regulations have a tendency to morph into protections for existing providers and for inefficient supply-chain participants with little incentive to innovate.

That seems to be the case with taxi and limousine services. Rather than competing by offering better tools themselves, the regulated incumbents have so far focused their response on efforts to ban the new services. State and local regulators are being urged to declare Uber and others in violation of decades-old laws outlawing unlicensed ride services, often basing their arguments on technical definitions of "meters," "dispatch," and "taxi."

In many cases, detractors of the new services have resorted to disinformation campaigns, falsely telling consumers that drivers dispatched through Uber are either unlicensed or uninsured—even dangerous.

The strategy has worked in some cities, if only temporarily. In its short life, Uber has spent more of its time litigating than innovating, fighting fines and in some cases outright bans in San Francisco, Chicago, Massachusetts, New York, Washington, D.C., and Toronto. Uber can't operate in Miami, for example, where existing laws prohibit limos from picking up passengers less than an hour after receiving a reservation, and requiring a minimum fare of $80.

The start-ups, however, have increasingly powerful counterweapons at their disposal: the fanatical devotion of early users, who utilize the power of near-perfect market information to lobby regulators in ways that can be even more effective than the efforts of the incumbents.

In Washington, D.C., and San Francisco, for example, intervention by Uber customers scored dramatic reversals. Rather than spend money they don't have on lobbyists of their own, ride-sharing startups are mobilizing a vocal army of loyal users who use social networks, blogs, and other online media to spread the word when threats appear.

In many cases, customers actually show up at city council and public utility commission meetings to defend the disrupters, unprecedented behavior that clearly catches regulators off guard and throws them into near-panic. Most have little direct experience dealing with the public whose interests they are charged with protecting. In some cities, regulatory bans and stiff penalties have been replaced by promises from the regulators to liberalize if not to rethink entirely the rationale behind tightly regulated paid ride services.

Room-sharing service Airbnb, which survived its scaling crisis, is now fighting claims that it operates an unauthorized hotel service and is evading the collection of hospitality taxes. There are also increasing legal actions being taken against individuals who list their apartments, either for violating the terms of their leases or local laws that, while difficult if not impossible to enforce, theoretically attach hefty fines to such behavior.

Disruption has clearly gotten ahead of the law. In New York City, as many as thirty thousand residents are registered Airbnb hosts, generating an estimated $1 billion in revenue for the city's tourism business. But these hosts may be violating a 2010 law that prohibits turning apartments into hotels, a law that was originally passed, ironically, to stop landlords from converting residential buildings into more profitable temporary lodgings.

At a conference on the importance of industrial design in creating disruptive innovations, Airbnb's CEO Brian Chesky concisely summed up the impact of bullet time on his company:

> We're navigating a world of very uncertain and fragmented laws in many cities. We have to think broadly and very differently and holistically about government relations. It's not just about meeting with government officials. It's about solving a design problem—if we have problems in governments, that's a design problem we need to solve.

More to the point, slowing the inevitable can easily backfire, as the reversals achieved by ride-sharing services and other "barely legal by design" innovations demonstrate. Bullet time should be utilized with extreme caution, and never in isolation. At best, it buys you time to catch up, not to declare victory. When legal logjams are broken, the pressure for Big Bang change is often that much more intense. Deferred adoption often becomes more sudden and more complete.

What happens after Big Bang Disruptors, driven by near-perfect market information, have reached saturation? We'll look at that in the next stage of the shark fin, the Big Crunch. First, we need to take a coffee break. A disruptive coffee break, as it turns out.

CHAPTER 6
THE BIG CRUNCH
THE INNOVATOR'S NIGHTMARE

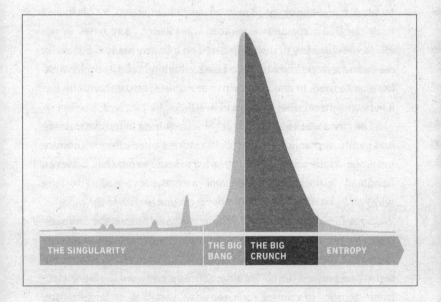

THE SINGULARITY | THE BIG BANG | THE BIG CRUNCH | ENTROPY

Starbucks was nearly a victim of its own innovation.

The ubiquitous coffee chain was growing at a phenomenal pace through much of last decade. In 1987, the company had only seventeen stores, but by 1999 the number had grown to twenty-five hundred. That total doubled and redoubled until 2007.

Then, with more than fifteen thousand company-operated coffee shops worldwide, the company's growth hit a wall. Day-to-day store traffic stalled for the first time in the company's forty-year history, and Starbucks began closing locations (mostly in the United States) at roughly the same pace it was opening them. By the end of the year, the company's stock had lost over 40 percent of its value.

Legendary CEO Howard Schultz returned to rescue the company he had built. Schultz set to work refocusing the stores on providing a premium experience to match its premium prices. The former, he thought, had been lost in all the growth.

The source of much of the company's troubles was disruptive technology—technology pioneered and championed by Starbucks itself. As U.S. consumers embraced the idea of daily lattes in the 1980s, the company first standardized on a largely manual European espresso machine known as the Linea, a high-tech, low-profile workhorse with room to make six drinks at a time. (The company still has a version at its original location in Seattle.)

The Linea was an artisan's machine, requiring extensive training and plenty of practice before it could deliver a consistently superior beverage. As the company's success led to faster expansion, however, handmade espresso drinks became a bottleneck, leading to long waits and vast differences in quality from one barista to the next.

So in 2000, near the end of Schultz's original tenure, the company began switching out its twenty thousand Linea machines, replacing them with the semiautomatic Verismo 801. The Verismo ground the beans and pressed the coffee automatically, and used the latest electronic sensors to control such sensitive variables as temperature, humidity, and even barometric pressure. The Verismo offered fast, consistent performance with minimal training, helping to fuel the company's explosive growth.

But if a quality espresso drink could be made by a machine, why would consumers continue to pay for handcrafting? Amazed by the margins Starbucks was earning on its products, fast-food giants including McDonald's and Dunkin' Donuts adopted similar technology, producing espresso drinks that, according to some reviewers, were just as good but considerably cheaper.

In 2007, McDonald's announced plans to expand McCafé, its café-within-a-restaurant, by adding espresso machines to the majority of its fourteen thousand U.S. locations. McDonald's uses super-automated espresso makers that not only grind the beans, but also tamp them to the proper density, run water through at the perfect temperature, and then steam the milk and add it to the drink. These "bean to cup" machines, as one vending operator bluntly put it, "replicate a barista providing a varied coffee menu, without the cost of actually hiring one."

Starbucks responded to its new competitors by imitating them, increasing its menu of breakfast sandwiches and installing even more drive-through windows.

That was enough to make Schultz's blood boil. He had opposed the breakfast sandwiches all along, and particularly hated the smell of singed cheddar cheese that had come to permeate the stores. "Where was the magic in burnt cheese?" he wrote in a scathing memo to the Starbucks board. The stores, he said, had squandered their "romance and theater," and the company had "lost its soul." While Schultz acknowledged that many of the company's decisions were necessary to achieve scale, they had inadvertently commoditized the idea of high-end coffee and made it easy for others with the same technology to undercut Starbucks. When the memo went public, the board surrendered, and asked Schultz to save its foundering empire.

Schultz refocused the company on innovation. His seven-point transformational agenda included closing six hundred U.S. stores, and retraining each of the company's 135,000 employees. Store layouts were varied to give them "the warm feeling of a neighborhood store." Expansion was scaled back.

Most visibly, Schultz threw out the Verismos, replacing them with a modernist-designed machine with a soft-colored metal finish and a giant flying saucer top where the premium beans are prominently visible. There is less automation in the new technology, giving baristas control over grind size, pour time, and the steaming of the milk. At seven inches shorter than its predecessor, the new machine also makes it possible once again for customers to watch their drinks being made and to interact with the barista.

Schultz's plan appears to have saved the company. Starbucks has reestablished itself as a premium brand, selling not just its coffee but the experience of its locations, the artistry of its employees, and the strength of its constant innovation. Though the number of company-operated stores has largely flattened since his return, revenue is rising at the same pace it was before the crisis. (See Figure 18.)

The crisis at Starbucks was a crisis of Big Bang proportions. The company trained consumers to indulge themselves in premium espresso drinks and pioneered disruptive innovations that allowed a labor-intensive operation to scale like an exponential technology.

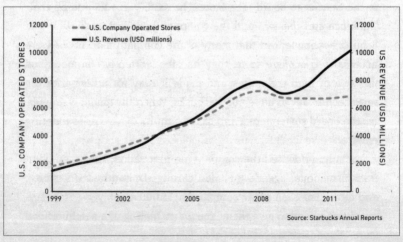

FIGURE 18. Starbucks Escapes the Big Crunch

As new competitors began to use that same technology against the company, however, the market became saturated ahead of Starbucks's carefully planned schedule.

At the same time, the company failed to anticipate what consumers would want next. Innovation turned to imitation. Growth stalled; revenue declined. Starbucks was caught in a trap.

We call that trap the Big Crunch. In the Big Bang stage, the market explodes and then expands dramatically in response to the introduction of a winning combination of innovative technologies and business models. As Big Bang markets become saturated, however, they implode. While the Big Bang stage is filled with excitement and exuberance, the Big Crunch is the sober morning after. As we shall see, it is the most dangerous stage of the shark fin.

Starbucks narrowly escaped the natural tendency of successful innovators to be smothered by their own success. Many once high-flying companies aren't so fortunate. Start-ups and incumbents alike are frequently caught unprepared for the rapid market saturation that occurs when near-perfect market information brings every interested customer to their door all at once, to be quickly served either by them or aggressive imitators.

In their exuberance they also often overlook the unpredictable tastes of increasingly faddish consumers, whose preferences can shift overnight in the opposite direction. With the arrival of a better and cheaper alternative, abandonment can be spontaneous, even immediate. Markets that once took years and even decades to saturate can now reach their natural capacity in months or weeks.

In the hyper-fast world of Japanese consumer electronics, for example, mobile carriers are pressing device manufacturers to provide new models every few months. For Sony, which hopes to rescue its struggling electronics business with a pivot to mobile devices, the shrinking life cycle is adding enormous pressure.

The company's wildly popular Xperia Z, a smart phone released in early 2013, sold more than six hundred thousand units in its first ten weeks. A few months later, however, consumers had moved on and in June of that year Sony stopped making the Xperia Z. The company was left scrambling for something new to offer Japanese consumers before it even had the chance to launch the Xperia Z in other markets.

Sony's challenge is hardly unusual. In every market driven by exponential technologies, the life cycle of Big Bang Disruptors is short and bittersweet.

That kind of shifting fortune is the result of what we call "the line of sudden death." (See Figure 19.) In markets driven by exponential technologies, the shift from one S-curve of disruptive new product and service adoption to the next happens not only more quickly but often before incumbents have fully amortized their investments in

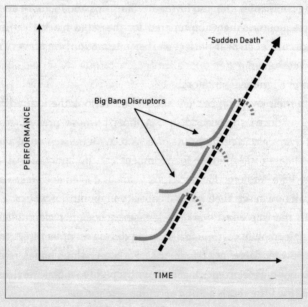

FIGURE 19. The Line of Sudden Death

the previous generation of disruptors. Even before reaching the top of one S-curve, customers leap to the bottom of the next, often destroying industry supply chains and risking the survival of participants used to having more time to adapt. Those who can't join their customers in making the leap disappear, and quickly.

When the Big Crunch comes, markets contract, pulling down start-ups and incumbents alike. Related industries can also be devastated. Hard-earned profits are at risk of being dissipated as markets collapse. Worse, investor confidence often shifts faster than the market. As stakeholders run for the exits, market value is destroyed, and with it the flexibility to make strategic decisions.

For those who manage to soldier on, strategy shifts dramatically in the Big Crunch. Here it's all about survival of the fastest—the fastest to recognize impending market saturation, the fastest to scale down, and the fastest to shed assets that are soon to become liabilities. To compete with undisciplined competitors, incumbents must prepare for immediate evacuation of current markets and be ready to liquidate core holdings—factories, distribution networks, inventory, and intellectual property.

The winners are invariably companies that know how to temper exuberance over Big Bang success with the pragmatic reality that the party can't and won't last long. They know when saturation is near, and avoid getting caught with excess inventory and strategic assets that quickly turn to liabilities. They shed mature technologies doomed to obsolescence, and do so before they become worthless.

Success in the Big Crunch depends on moving quickly enough to escape the line of sudden death. Companies that survive this stage already know how to jump the S-curve from one set of disruptive technologies to the next. Incumbents who use this stage to reinvent themselves as more agile and more profitable competitors, on the other hand, are those who can jump . . . straight up.

How to do it? Success in the Big Crunch requires very different skills and expertise than the previous stages. You'll need to pivot quickly, moving from rapid growth to timely exit, jettisoning anything that doesn't help you transition to the next cycle of innovation.

The three rules for this, the razor-sharp edge of the shark fin, are all about moving faster than the crunch: to avoid committing capital and resources just before the bust, including to short-lived inventory; to avoid stranding assets and infrastructure investments; and finally, to avoid stranding profits.

Rule 7. *Anticipate Saturation*—When consumers adopt and then abandon new products and services all at once, it's essential not to be caught with excess capacity or inventory. You need to anticipate saturation before it happens and to scale down as quickly as you scaled up. Poorly timed purchases—whether of raw materials, inventories, or of companies whose value is about to peak—can wreak havoc with your balance sheet.

Rule 8. *Shed Assets Before They Become Liabilities*—As one generation of disruptors fades, related assets—factories, distribution networks, and intellectual property—can lose value, gradually and then suddenly. Knowing the right time to sell, and to whom, can mean the difference between your ability to develop the next disruptor and bankruptcy. Knowing which assets to keep for the next cycle of innovation is equally important.

Rule 9. *Quit While You're Ahead*—Even if—especially if—you've dominated your industry for decades. The replacement of core technologies with new disruptors can wipe out all your retained earnings quickly if you allow it to. Courageous executives accept the inevitable, and announce their exit from current markets while they are still strong. Doing so gives you more time to move to a new ecosystem. Even better, it forces competitors to change on your schedule.

RULE 7. ANTICIPATE SATURATION

To survive the Big Bang, as we said in Chapter Five, you need to scale up quickly. To preserve your profits in the Big Crunch, you also need to know when and how to scale down, sometimes even faster.

Unfortunately, many innovators refuse to believe the end has come at all, let alone so soon. Dramatic, even fanatic market adoption of your disruptor may fill you with confidence and a sense of invulnerability. But even as near-perfect market information giveth, it inevitably taketh away. If you're not careful, all the value you built up in the explosive growth of the Big Bang can be lost just as fast in the Big Crunch.

To avoid that fate, you'll need detailed data and sophisticated analytic tools to predict the shape of sales demand, particularly to know the point at which sales are likely to dramatically drop off—the point of no return. Make no mistake: The popularity of Big Bang Disruptors always drops off quickly, either because their target markets become quickly saturated or because the next better and cheaper alternative arrives ahead of (your) schedule.

Perhaps no example captures the risk of misjudging the shape of market demand and the timing of market saturation so poignantly as the story of Zynga, the once high-flying mobile gaming company.

Zynga made its name early with a wildly popular Facebook social game called Farmville. As Farmville's popularity faded and relations with Facebook became tense, Zynga began looking for new disruptors. It found one, or so it seemed, in a small game studio called OMGPOP.

After running through nearly all of a $16 million investment from venture financing its founders had raised, OMGPOP had little to show for its efforts. But in early 2012, OMGPOP struck gold with Draw Something, an online version of an old board game called Pictionary.

Draw Something users were given a randomly selected word and asked to create an illustration that was sent over the Internet to another player, who needed to guess the word before sending back an illustration of his own.

Draw Something offered just the right recipe of competitiveness, community, and entertainment necessary to become seriously addictive. After only nine days, the game had a million active users. For several days thereafter, the number of participants continued to double every day.

Draw Something became a cultural meme—something that everyone was talking about. Seven weeks after its launch, the game had been downloaded thirty-five million times. Adoption was so rapid that OMGPOP's external hosting service couldn't handle the volume, and game performance began to suffer. A small team of engineers stayed up for days to rewrite the game's back-end software, and then pulled off a late-night move to dedicated servers, which ultimately numbered close to a hundred.

Zynga knew a good thing when it saw it, and swooped in with impressive efficiency. Rather than simply license the game, Zynga acquired OMGPOP, closing a deal less than a month after the launch of Draw Something. The purchase price was an astonishing $180 million—$4.5 million per OMGPOP employee or $15 per active Draw Something user, depending on how you looked at it.

Despite Zynga's speed, the acquisition came too late. As Figure 20 shows, Draw Something's user base peaked only days after the merger. The market, it turns out, was nearly saturated. It soon became bored. After reaching fifteen million active users in a matter of weeks, a month later Draw Something was down to ten million players. A few months later, the number had collapsed to two million. Users moved on, switching en masse from Draw Something to a different game from another developer—a new version of Angry Birds.

After almost vertical growth, Draw Something hit the line of

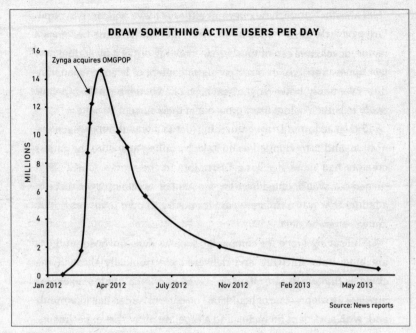

FIGURE 20. Bad Timing: Draw Something, from Big Bang to Big Crunch

sudden death. By itself, the inevitable saturation wouldn't have been fatal had OMGPOP's developers been ready with a new title. Unfortunately, OMGPOP couldn't re-create the magic. Culture clashes dogged the merged company. Zynga soon wrote down its investment in OMGPOP by half and then, a year after the acquisition, simply closed the studio altogether.

By early 2013, Zynga announced its revenue had dropped nearly 66 percent from the previous year; a few months later, Zynga laid off 20 percent of its staff. By then, daily and monthly active users for the company had fallen to their lowest levels in over two years. Zynga's market value plummeted from a high of nearly $9 billion to only $2 billion just a year later.

Mobile games, much like Hollywood movies, often operate in a "blockbuster" mode; new offerings either achieve widespread popularity or little to no notice at all. Once a winning game becomes a meme, developers can often squeeze more life out of it by adding new levels, new versions, or other premium content or licensed merchandise. Eventually, however, the next big hit had better be in the pipeline, ready to launch before users grow out of their current favorite.

Zynga acquired Draw Something just as it was about to reach saturation, and compounded its mistake by failing to ensure the game's creators had more Big Bang Disruptors in the works. OMGPOP, it turned out, was doomed from the moment of its catastrophic success, a failure that was ultimately paid for not by its own investors but by Zynga's shareholders.

The saving grace for companies such as Zynga, whose products are built from software and delivered electronically through the cloud, is that when saturation does lead to crunch, there's no excess inventory to depreciate or liquidate. The enterprise can lick its wounds and, with sufficient financing and a pipeline of market experiments, move on to the next disruptor. Zynga, which hired Microsoft's senior gaming executive as its CEO in mid-2013, may yet recover.

Surviving saturation is harder, however, for companies whose goods take physical form. For them, the pain of saturation has an extra kick—the possibility of being caught with warehouses of items that consumers no longer want—at any price. Long-term sourcing contracts and lead times for distribution encourage companies to build production schedules with plenty of cushion, particularly if there's a chance of catastrophic success. Doing so, however, reduces the company's flexibility. When markets suddenly shift in the other direction, reversing course is that much harder.

The line of sudden death between Big Bang and Big Crunch creates a whipsaw. Producers who want to capture early profits (often the only kind available) must produce enough inventory to satisfy explosive demand for market experiments that take off. Yet failing to predict—or at least to insure against—the risk of building too much product can wipe out everything gained in a matter of days when customers suddenly lose interest.

Consider the Barnes & Noble Nook. Released in 2009 to compete with Amazon's Kindle, the Nook initially looked like a winner for the bookstore chain, selling sixty thousand units in its first year and gaining about 20 percent of the fast-growing market for e-book readers. But as new models of the Kindle from Amazon, along with book-reading apps for the Apple iPad and Android-based tablets gained momentum, the high-flying Nook faced increasingly stiff competition.

In mid-2013, quarterly losses from the Nook topped $177 million, over $130 million of which was associated with write-downs on excess inventory. While Amazon's e-book revenues continue to grow, sales at traditional bookstores continue to fall. The content business, it seems, has shifted industries—from brick-and-mortar retailers to technology companies. Remaining bookstores have been backed into an ever-tighter corner.

The Big Crunch can hit even harder for makers of peripheral products and services that add on to the Big Bang Disruptors of others. Manufacturers of supporting products and services may have less insight into the direction of an ecosystem than those who produce the core products.

All the manufacturing flexibility in the world is of little use to producers that can't anticipate the repolarized gravity of the Big Crunch—or refuse to believe such a change is even possible. That's the moral of the story in the dramatic rise and fall of THQ, a California-based game developer driven to liquidation by its colossal failure to spot imminent saturation for its most successful product.

In 2010, THQ created uDraw, an innovative drawing tablet for use with the Nintendo Wii. uDraw users can draw or paint on the device and see their creations appear on their television screen. The device was integrated into games, such as Wii's electronic version of Pictionary, and used with stand-alone drawing programs such as THQ's own uDraw Studio. Either way, uDraw was a hit. After shipping more than a million tablets in just three months, the company proudly announced plans to sell similar devices for use in other game platforms, including Microsoft's Xbox and Sony's PlayStation.

In the few months the company needed to ramp up production of the new models, however, THQ found itself face-to-face with a better and cheaper competitor: Apple's iPad. The enthusiastic reception for Apple's stand-alone tablet, which offered its own suite of drawing games and apps, greatly diminished demand for add-on drawing devices for game consoles. By the time uDraw for the Xbox and PlayStation was launched, few third-party game developers were interested in integrating it into their products.

The iPad had accelerated market saturation for uDraw on all three consoles, but THQ inexplicably kept producing the device. In 2012, the company was caught with an unsold inventory of 1.4 million tablets, nearly as many as it had sold. The result was a revenue shortfall, in just one quarter, of $100 million. The company quickly replaced its management team, which expressed shock at what it considered one of the biggest mistakes in the history of the video gaming industry. "I'm not sure how that happened," the company's new head of development bluntly told a trade publication.

Stunned by a market jump on the line of sudden death, THQ never recovered. By late 2012, the company had declared bankruptcy and was facing investor lawsuits. When creditors rejected a restructuring plan, THQ's game titles and other intellectual property—the company's only remaining assets—were sold at auction.

Capital-intensive or "durable" goods may experience saturation more slowly, but the consequences of missing the warning signs are often more dramatic. By definition, customers keep durable goods, including large appliances and cars, long after their initial purchase.

Here, the shift from Big Bang to Big Crunch may not be the result so much of short-lived fads and fashions as more subtle long-term changes in demographics and shifts in social attitudes.

These, in any case, appear to be the real causes of wrenching transformations over the last decade in the nearly $1 trillion worldwide automobile industry. While the economic downturn that began in 2007 accelerated the shift to more fuel-efficient and environmentally responsible vehicles, consumers and business customers had already been moving in that direction for years.

Some automakers, including Ford and Nissan, appear to have heeded the warnings of industry truth-tellers who warned of these changes. Others did not. Consider the near-death experience of automotive pioneer GM, which, from 1931 to 2007, sold more cars than any other automaker for a remarkable seventy-seven-year run.

Yet despite having brilliantly navigated the Great Depression, World War II, and other historic and economic upheavals, the company, with more than 280,000 employees, nearly disappeared. GM's precipitous 2009 fall into bankruptcy and its government-backed rescue is perhaps the most dramatic story we have of the capricious fortunes even the most established companies face in the Big Crunch.

While many factors—internal as well as external—contributed to the company's meltdown, a repeated failure to recognize saturation was a contributor.

A good example is GM's delayed decision to sell its Hummer brand. Once a darling of the rich and famous, the tanklike Hummer H1, with its $130,000 sticker price and appalling fuel efficiency, came to symbolize waste and excess. Despite the 2005 introduction of radically scaled-down Hummer H3, Hummer's doom was clear well before GM's bankruptcy.

But management held on to the unit, hoping somehow to resurrect or, if not, then to sell it to a possible buyer in China. After continued losses, GM finally decided to sell, but not until 2010. By then, not surprisingly, there were no buyers. The company was forced to steeply discount a remaining two thousand unsold vehicles and liquidate the unit.

Complicating the problem of market saturation, car makers facing extinction can't simply shut down once the crunch becomes unbearable. Depending on the market, manufacturers maintain a legal obligation to provide warranty and spare parts for as much as a decade after liquidation. (GM is still making parts for Oldsmobile, for example, which ceased production in 2004.) That makes it harder, on the one hand, to find a buyer and, on the other, simply to give up.

RULE 8. SHED ASSETS BEFORE THEY BECOME LIABILITIES

Avoiding the potentially fatal mistake of stranded inventory is only the first rule of survival in the Big Crunch. You also need to rid yourself of factories, equipment, and other property that may no longer be strategic, and whose value is likely to decline in parallel with declining markets. As customers shift to the next disruptor, even core assets devaluate rapidly, transforming cruelly into liabilities.

One way to minimize the risk of stranded assets is to own as few of them as possible, following the example of lean start-ups. Thanks to exponential technology, it has become easier than ever to efficiently outsource functions, resources, and infrastructure and still maintain quality and future flexibility.

Production may be outsourced to developing markets, for example, and infrastructure leased on demand from cloud-based providers, including application processing such as accounting, distribution, and customer systems. If you've concentrated your efforts on combinatorial innovation and market experiments, shedding assets in the Big Crunch may be relatively painless—perhaps just the cancellation of short-term contracts for production, distribution, and the licensing of intellectual property.

Running lean is by no means a strategy reserved for start-ups and entrepreneurs. As exponential technologies relentlessly drive down the transaction costs of every manner of market interaction, even large-scale manufacturing companies find they can operate with fewer owned assets. Sports-apparel giant Nike, for example, contracts with more than nine hundred manufacturing partners around the world, nearly half in Asia. The company claims its lean and sustainable production has reduced defect rates by 50 percent and lead times by 40 percent, even as productivity has risen 10 to 20 percent. As a result, revenue per employee is now more than half a million dollars.

For assets you still own, however, it's time for a sober reevaluation. Many, even some that were the source of your competitive advantage only months or weeks ago, will no longer be needed. The sooner you figure that out, the higher the price you can command. In the Big Crunch, your goal is to optimize the return on residual assets, either by selling them to competitors that lack your good sense of timing or to buyers in other industries that can put them to new uses, perhaps even to recombine them into new disruptors.

In public companies, chief financial officers have long been evaluated on their ability to acquire just the right resources to satisfy unmet customer needs. Few CFOs, however, are expert at returning those resources back to the market at optimal prices. But given the short life span of Big Bang Disruptors and the harsh realities of the Big Crunch, an ability to maximize return on residual assets will ultimately determine, when all is said and done, whether even successful market experiments actually generate net profits.

In that regard, executives should emulate the wisdom of Corning, the serial disrupter behind Gorilla Glass, the ubiquitous technology protecting the displays of more than 1.5 billion smartphones and other devices. Gorilla Glass combines thinness, lightness, and damage resistance, the perfect protection for our proliferating screens.

In 1952, a failed experiment at Corning's upstate New York research facility led to the intriguing possibility that glass fired at higher temperatures could prove more resilient. At the time, the company couldn't identify a market for the technology, and filed the project away. Decades later, Apple founder Steve Jobs approached Corning in 2007 with a need for a durable, high-quality display protector for the company's soon-to-be-released iPhone. Corning dusted off its research and, in a matter of months, had adapted both the technology and its manufacturing facilities to make Gorilla Glass work at scale.

The results have been profound. By 2013, Gorilla Glass was being used in more than seven hundred and fifty products, from mobile devices to high-end televisions. Sales have grown from $20 million in 2007 to $1 billion in 2012. And Corning has constantly enhanced the product based on detailed analyses of customer mishaps and breakage, increasing its strength by 20 percent for Gorilla Glass 2.0.

An even better version is in the works. Yet, Corning CEO Wendell Weeks is too smart to expect his big hit will top the charts forever. Early market experiments are already proliferating that could revolutionize display technology, including alternatives based on organic LED technology, or OLED. The promise of OLED, an exponential technology, includes both lower cost and better performance—OLED will support ever-higher concentrations of pixels, enabling higher definition displays. Some believe that OLEDs will soon be flexible enough to be rolled up and stored.

Corning understands the risk to Gorilla Glass from OLED. The company, in fact, is one of the leading OLED experimenters—working with Samsung, for example, in the development of an OLED display it calls Lotus Glass. That hedge softens the blow of knowing that no matter how successful Gorilla Glass is today, it will someday be eclipsed—at least in its current markets.

So at the height of Big Bang adoption, Corning is already planning second and third lives for its core technology and the manufacturing capacity currently dedicated to its production. The company announced in 2013 that it was developing a version of Gorilla Glass that could replace traditional windshields in automobiles, where the lighter weight of Gorilla Glass could improve fuel efficiency even as it offers better resistance to scratches and chips.

The company has already signed up a major car company to try out the idea, perhaps as early as 2014. If Corning can produce a windshield that is both better and cheaper, it could in turn signal Big Bang Disruption for traditional windshield makers, an estimated $3 billion business.

Corning's careful planning contrasts sharply with bankrupt movie-rental chain Blockbuster Video, which failed to recognize in time the threat to its brick-and-mortar business posed by virtual rental services such as Netflix. Few thought at the time of Netflix's launch that consumers would trade the convenience of picking up their videos to waiting for them to arrive by mail.

Users, however, embraced the automated self-service of Netflix's Web-based interface, technology that positioned the start-up to transition from mailing DVDs to streaming content over the Internet. As exponential technologies improved broadband speed, reliability, and adoption, Netflix transitioned in just a few years to a cloud-based service.

Blockbuster tried to follow each of Netflix's strategic moves, but remained a perennial second in the winner-take-all market for new ways to distribute entertainment content. Blockbuster fell further behind, weighed down by the high labor and real estate costs of its once-dominant physical locations—assets that became liabilities. In

2011, after closing some nine hundred stores, the company declared bankruptcy.

In the end, Blockbuster's assets were acquired for only $320 million by satellite television maverick Dish Networks, which was principally interested in Blockbuster's online channel and its 3.3 million customers. Had Blockbuster sold itself earlier, or found a way to shed the physical assets sooner, that price might have been much higher. In 1999, the year Netflix launched its online subscription service, Blockbuster was valued at close to $3 billion—nearly ten times what Dish ultimately paid.

The examples of Corning and Blockbuster suggest another important lesson about shedding assets. Timing is crucial, but so is finding the perfect buyer. Even if customers have lost interest in current technologies, there may be other companies in other ecosystems who can still put them to profitable use. Finding the company that can most efficiently squeeze out residual value translates to a higher sale price.

That's the moral of Google's acquisition of Motorola Mobility, the consumer division of the former radio pioneer. After a series of missteps in the migration from analog to digital standards, in early 2011 Motorola separated into two different companies. Motorola Solutions continued the company's historic role providing radio equipment for government, public safety, and enterprise customers. Motorola Mobility took over the struggling consumer device business.

Only months after the creation of Motorola Mobility, Google made a surprise offer to acquire the company for $12.5 billion, a 5 percent premium over its market value. Google's buyout of Motorola Mobility was clearly motivated by a desire for new devices to showcase Google's Android operating system. But Google's price also reflected an interest in the residual value of Motorola's intellectual property, particularly its remarkable portfolio of seventeen thousand active patents and another seventy-five hundred pending approval.

The patents were of considerable worth to Motorola, which needed them to protect the company in the increasingly litigious global smartphone ecosystem. Google, which had been fighting its own patent war over Android, needed them more. At the time of its acquisition of Motorola Mobility, Google had already spent hundreds of millions of dollars to defend itself from multiple lawsuits. Losing any one of them could have meant the end of Google's growing dominance in the mobile universe.

Google had lost out in an earlier auction for the patents of defunct Canadian telecommunications giant Nortel, which were sold instead to a group of companies including Apple, Microsoft, Sony, Ericsson, and EMC. Rumors were circulating that Microsoft was also interested in Motorola.

Google acknowledged that it had significant interest in the patents, telling analysts at the time of the Motorola acquisition, "We think that having this kind of patent portfolio to protect the ecosystem is a good thing." Underscoring Motorola's true value, Google laid off four thousand Motorola employees—roughly 20 percent of the total workforce—soon after the acquisition, and shuttered about a third of the division's ninety locations.

Had Motorola recognized in time that the patents were worth more to someone else in the rapidly evolving mobile ecosystem, the company might have realized an even better deal, and sooner. Rather than allowing itself to get caught in the Big Crunch, Motorola would have been better off looking for a buyer earlier in the shark fin.

As this example makes clear, the proactive disposal of residual assets is a particularly attractive strategy for intellectual property, particularly for patents. Patents don't have to be sold on an exclusive basis—they can also be licensed. Doing so allows both buyer and seller to make optimal use of the same assets. Licensing deals can even be structured to shift ownership over time, transferring the asset as the seller's needs decline and the buyer's increase.

The residual value of patents played a similar role in the endgame of film-based photography, particularly in the fate of Kodak.

As Big Bang Disruption transformed photography from an analog to a digital industry, Kodak famously missed its chance to translate dominance in film into a starring role in the expanding world of digital imagery. Kodak invented the first digital camera in the 1970s, but was never comfortable with the lower margins of better and cheaper digital photography. By the time Kodak was ready to commit to all-digital devices, cameras were rapidly being replaced with smart-phones, leaving Kodak few options to leverage its brand.

After years of falling revenue, Kodak entered bankruptcy in 2012, a move that was intended to give the company a chance to capitalize on its substantial digital assets without the baggage of its long history as a film pioneer. Investors said no. After over a century of operation, during much of which the company owned one of the most valuable brands in the world, most of Kodak's remaining assets were sold, and

FIGURE 21. Kodak Goes Bankrupt Gradually and then Suddenly

for a fraction of their onetime value. As Figure 21 shows, Kodak had gone bankrupt, gradually and then suddenly.

In bankruptcy, the most attractive asset, not surprisingly, proved to be Kodak's portfolio of eleven hundred digital imaging and processing patents. While the company hadn't leveraged those inventions well enough to survive, the trustees nonetheless expected that Kodak's intellectual property still held considerable residual value. They offered to sell the patents for $2.5 billion. But the winning bid, from a group of buyers that included Apple, Google, and Facebook, came in at only a little over half a billion.

Had Kodak, like Motorola, waited too long to get the best price? Perhaps not. According to *Wired*'s Sarah Mitroff, documents filed in the bankruptcy proceeding showed that Kodak had already earned $3 billion from licensing those patents—licenses that continued after the sale. What's more, Mitroff notes, "Those licensing fees made up a significant part of Kodak's revenue" in the years before the company closed its doors.

Selling orphaned intellectual property to buyers outside the photography business may have been the best possible outcome for Kodak, whose longtime dominance of the U.S. photography market seemed to paralyze management when the Big Crunch finally came. It was hardly the ending George Eastman could have imagined when he founded the company as a technology and business pioneer in 1888. In 2013, what was left of the company emerged from bankruptcy, hoping to transform itself into a supplier of commercial imaging for other businesses.

RULE 9. QUIT WHILE YOU'RE AHEAD

Avoiding stranded inventory and depreciating assets, including intellectual property, only gets you so far in the Big Crunch. As markets begin their inevitable decline, the bigger risk for both entrepreneurs and incumbents alike is losing more money than they made in the previous stages, including war chests and emergency funds saved up over decades.

Protecting your profits demands close attention to the previous two rules in this chapter. Fire-sale prices for unneeded inventory on the one hand and wasted production capacity on the other are sure-fire ways to drain away all the prior winnings from your successful disruptors.

There's more work to be done. Much of the infrastructure you built to support catastrophic growth can't be easily reduced, even as the Big Crunch inevitably proceeds. You still need to maintain your network of retail locations, Web sites, and service contracts. Factories and offices must be maintained even when nothing is being produced. While you can advertise in fewer markets or with less frequency, the development of marketing collateral costs the same whether you are speaking to an audience of a billion or a thousand. Warranties may extend the life of obsolete products years after fixing them has ceased to be cost-effective.

Many of your customers can easily abandon one set of products for the next Big Bang Disruptor. Yet the cost of serving the remaining users do not, as a general rule, scale down proportionally. So even as new disruptors get better and cheaper, older products become worse and more expensive.

As the Big Crunch proceeds, products reaching the end of their life cycle become, perversely, more expensive to produce, distribute, and service—costs that accelerate as the number of users dwindles. Catastrophic success in the Big Bang likely required the rapid construction of a vast supporting ecosystem. So the bigger the early success of the fading product, the faster its abandonment can drain retained earnings.

Where Big Bang adoption generates economies of scale, Big Crunch abandonment saddles you with its opposite—diseconomies of scale. In the Big Bang, innovators experience virtuous cycles; in the Big Crunch, these reverse, becoming vicious. It's this depressing feature that makes the line of sudden death, well, sudden. Once you're caught in the downward spiral, there's little chance of escape.

To protect your cash reserves, you may need to engage the most counterintuitive idea we've yet described. You may need to kill off your existing business now, before the next generation of early market experiments shows even the faintest potential of generating a Big Bang Disruptor.

This is not a strategy for the faint of heart. Announcing the end of life for a core technology means ceding hard-fought market share to traditional competitors, which are left baffled by your seemingly unprovoked surrender ahead of any significant challenge, internal or external. Stock analysts may pillory your judgment, and punish your stock. Investors may call for your head.

Yet we've already seen examples of such behavior in industries long dominated by exponential technologies. In Chapter Three, we noted how entertainment giant Nintendo regularly deemphasized the marketing of its most popular game consoles every few years, in part because both the company and its customers knew that Moore's Law had made possible better and cheaper replacements, either from Nintendo or someone else.

In the fiercely competitive market for smartphone operating systems, likewise, the average life of even a major release of Android, iOS, or Windows Phone 8 is now less than six months. There's little point for developers or consumers to get too attached to any one version. Easier just to retire them at the first sign of disruption.

Of course it is relatively easy for an Internet start-up or even a consumer electronics company to cavalierly kill off the current version of a product that will eventually—perhaps soon—be disrupted. The initial investment in infrastructure to support it may have been small, for one thing. And innovators know full well that, thanks to exponential technologies and their expertise in combinatorial innovation, the opportunity to launch the next better and cheaper model is just around the corner.

But what about industrial giants with decades of experience working with just one set of basic technologies, invented perhaps by the company's revered founders? For them, a soon-to-be obsolete innovation of yesteryear may provide much of today's profits and cash flow, funding the development of a diversified portfolio of more risky investments and innovations.

Management's challenge is acute. Right now, you are the world's leading provider of a product found in every home and business in the world, with annual revenues of roughly $5 billion and profits of over $400 million. Still, your best truth-tellers have made it clear: Despite surviving many scrapes with death and outlasting dozens of failed pretenders to your throne, this time there's nothing you can do. What then?

In the inspiring example of Dutch-based Philips Lighting, one of the world's oldest and largest industrial companies, the answer was to do the unthinkable: announce the end of its bestselling products. And to make the announcement a full decade before better and cheaper replacements were likely to arrive.

In 2006, Philips, which had been producing incandescent lightbulbs since 1891, was refreshingly direct, even blunt. "One key element must shift, and soon, in order to increase energy efficiency," the company wrote. "Inefficient and costly-to-operate incandescent lighting has to be eliminated."

Eliminated! Soon! Hardly the words one expects from a market leader speaking about its core product, especially one whose basic technology, which Philips helped to invent, had stabilized before World War I. Producers of incandescent lightbulbs had moved through a succession of product refinements in an orderly fashion for the better part of a century. These, however, were gradual moves from one S-curve to the next. Few technologies had held off truly disruptive innovation for so long.

Lightbulbs had long provided Philips a steady stream of profits. As recently as 2009, the company overall relied on its lighting division for 30 percent, or €7 billion of the company's total revenue of over €23 billion. Most of that 30 percent came from the sale of incandescent bulbs.

Still, the end was inevitable. Despite their ubiquity, incandescent bulbs are grossly inefficient, producing far more heat than light and wasting most of the energy they use. Over the last decade, a combination of increased environmental awareness and improvements in alternative lighting technologies have put increased pressure on manufacturers to abandon their most basic invention, originally credited to Thomas Edison in 1879 and long seen as one of the defining technologies of his century.

Since 2006, Philips and, later, its competitors, have not flinched from the task of disassembling their incandescent business, promoting instead alternative lighting technologies, including compact fluorescent and LED, which promise new capabilities and customization, longer life, and cheaper operation.

The urgency to retire incandescent lighting was also driven, as the company emphasized, by legal requirements. Partly in response to the 1997 Kyoto Protocol to the United Nations Framework Convention on Climate Change, national governments began putting pressure on companies to create more energy-efficient products. Under the Kyoto protocols, signed by nearly every UN member state, industrial countries have committed to significant reductions of greenhouse gases by 2020.

Lighting was an obvious candidate for improvement, both because of its widespread use and its inefficiency. According to Philips, European consumers were buying two billion bulbs every year, mostly for home use. The switch to more efficient alternatives was projected to save consumers as much as €8 billion annually, indirectly eliminating twenty million tons of greenhouse gases.

Even more important to Philips's calculations was the unforgiving math of exponential technology. By 2006, it was clear that within a decade improvements in compact fluorescent and LED technologies would lead to better and cheaper alternatives to incandescent lighting. LEDs in particular have been on the exponential path of better and cheaper improvement since the 1960s. According to what is known as Haitz's Law, the cost per unit of light provided by LEDs falls by a factor of ten every decade. At the same time, the amount of light generated per LED increases by a factor of twenty at a given wavelength.

Like computing equipment, LEDs become dramatically more efficient and less expensive over time. They also last longer than incandescent bulbs and don't contain dangerous pollutants such as mercury that raise the costs and risks of disposal.

Haitz's Law, first documented in 2000, made clear to Philips that the devastation of its incandescent business was only a matter of time. So Philips decided to preempt the obsolescence of its core technology, moving quickly to effect a revolution, both to preserve as much value as possible and, more important, to outrun competitors caught off guard by Philips's announcement.

Philips has since completed what the company's executives describe as "a radical transformation." That transformation began by accepting both the inevitability of and potential devastation from Big Bang Disruption in incandescent lighting, which Philips did early and with enthusiasm.

The company then gave customers a decade of advance warning, easing the transition for buyers as well as for Philips. The early warning also gave the company time to retire or sell old manufacturing capacity and retool other assets. Meanwhile, Philips forged deeper relationships with new suppliers for fluorescent and LED materials.

The company also worked to position itself for a leadership role in a new lighting ecosystem, one where replacement bulbs would play a smaller role in driving profits. In 2007, for example, Philips spent $4.3 billion to snap up five diversified companies in the lighting sector, including a leading U.S. maker of light fixtures. Recognizing that solid-state lighting will ultimately require consumers to purchase new fixtures and controls, Philips plans to supply not just bulbs but the entire next-generation lighting infrastructure.

At the same time, Philips took the lead in working with environmental NGOs and other civil society organizations to encourage national governments to *require* manufacturers to end the sale of incandescent bulbs. Doing so bought valuable brand equity for Philips as a leader in sustainable business. It also meant an orderly and coordinated retirement of the old supply chains, established and enforced by neutral regulators.

Not incidentally, encouraging national timetables also forced competitors to play by a schedule created by Philips, and deflected negative publicity for the change from the manufacturers to the regulators. With mandates in place, consumers saw the government as the entity forcing them to break old habits and adapt to new technologies—technologies some may not have wanted to embrace.

That strategy has been wildly successful. In Europe, a mandatory phaseout of incandescents was completed by the end of 2012. (Philips ended production well ahead of the required date.) Australia and Canada have also introduced phaseouts. In the United States, despite second thoughts by some lawmakers, new efficiency standards effectively banned 100-watt incandescents in 2012.

Philips not only anticipated the end of its technology; it actually caused it to happen sooner—on a schedule set not by disruptive entrepreneurs but by Philips. "Green" product sales in the lighting division have grown from almost €3 billion in 2008 to nearly €6 billion by 2012—nearly 70 percent of total sales for the division. The company and its NGO partners are calling for a complete changeover of the world's four billion lighting sockets by 2016.

Philips Lighting's transformation changed the potential for "sudden death" into leadership in early market experiments for disruptive lighting. The company's Hue product, for example, is an LED lighting system that allows users to control power, brightness, and even the color of individual bulbs from any mobile device. Hue can also be programmed to respond to preset alarms or events, such as receiving an e-mail from a particular sender.

Philips's business-killing initiative took genuine insight, courage, and senior management leadership. It included a decision to kill the company's oldest and highest-grossing business unit, announcing that decision to customers and competitors years ahead of the transition, and working with governments to force the company to stick to its commitment.

It sounds dangerous, and it was. But in the Big Crunch, the greater danger would have been simply to wait for alternative technologies to stumble their way into consumer homes, taking action only after the line of sudden death was clearly drawn.

Philips might easily have dug in its heels, denying the decline of a core technology even as disruptors were nipping at its heels. Instead of spearheading intrusive government regulation mandating major change to its business model, it might have taken the more conventional tack of using its significant worldwide political muscle to fight it tooth and nail.

And it could have kept making incandescent bulbs for a market that might have at first declined slowly, or even looked to be improving as weaker competitors dropped out. At some point, though, the decline would have gone from gradual to sudden, turning assets into liabilities and profits into losses. By then, it would have been too late to migrate to more promising markets.

Philips, like other successful practitioners of Big Bang Disruption, discovered in time that it needed to break all the old rules of business strategy. There can be little doubt that a more conventional approach would have meant lights out for one of the world's oldest brands.

Which seems to be the fate of an even older enterprise—one with a legal monopoly for its primary service that has lasted over two hundred years; a monopoly that, it turns out, is leading more quickly to doom than to salvation. That's the story we'll use to introduce the final stage of the shark fin: the cold, lonely future known as Entropy.

CHAPTER 7
ENTROPY
RIDING OFF INTO THE SUNSET

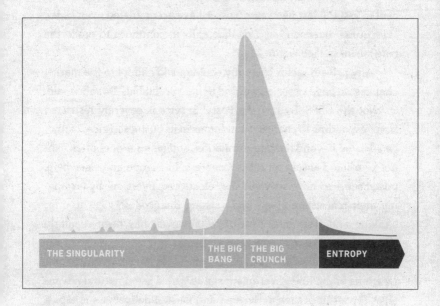

THE SINGULARITY   THE BIG BANG   THE BIG CRUNCH   ENTROPY

Neither snow nor rain nor heat nor gloom of night," according to the long-standing creed of the United States Postal Service, "stays these couriers from the swift completion of their appointed rounds."

Neither, it seems, does bankruptcy.

The USPS, a quasi-governmental corporation under the control of the U.S. government, technically went broke in 2012, when its debt grew to more than $15 billion, exceeding the borrowing limit set by Congress. That followed nearly a decade of losses, as nearly every measure of demand for service declined "precipitously," to use the word of Patrick Donahoe, the current postmaster general and chief executive officer of the $65 billion enterprise.

The Postal Service was confident of its future after surviving and even expanding during the early days of e-mail and other forms of electronic communications and content delivery. Starting in 2000, however, first-class mail began a dangerous descent, falling 29 percent in just the last five years. Losses have accumulated even faster. "Electronic diversion," as Donahoe calls it, continues to erode the core business. (See Figure 22.)

"Any private sector company could quickly adapt to the market changes we have experienced, and remain profitable," Donahoe said.

Not the USPS. By law, the Postal Service is severely restricted from responding to changing conditions in its business. Prices cannot be adjusted beyond the rate of inflation, and new services often cannot be offered absent an act of Congress. In Europe and elsewhere, postal services have survived the "electronic diversion" by leveraging their real estate assets and existing financial services to offer banking and insurance. The USPS, however, has been regularly denied the authority to make similar moves.

The post office can't even participate in digital communications, where its brand and government status would seem natural advantages for services such as verified and trusted delivery—perhaps a solution for the epidemic of spam e-mail. In 2012, Donahoe said only that the postal service was "Looking into new and emerging communications technology, like digital mail," and told Congress that the USPS had recently created a "Digital Solutions Group" tasked with "finding innovative ways to use technology to better meet customer needs."

The loss of business has accelerated the negative impacts of a

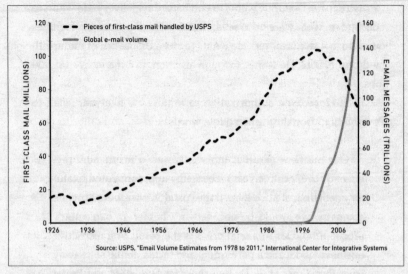

FIGURE 22. The Disruption of First-Class Mail

long history of poor strategic decisions, some by Congress. In 2006, for example, when the agency's nearly five hundred thousand employees were producing significant profits, Congress moved to prop up the federal government's troubled health care insurance program by requiring the USPS to prepay health care costs for its future retirees, pumping billions into the fund.

The prepayment requirement was set to last an astonishing seventy-five years. By 2010, the Postal Service had been forced by law to overfund the program by over $10 billion. Today, health care costs constitute 20 percent of every dollar of revenue the post office takes in, accounting for $7 billion of its annual shortfall. In 2012, USPS defaulted on a mandatory $11 billion payment to the fund.

The postmaster general has a plan, one that could put the service back in the black in just a few years. Most of the changes involve scaling back current services, network operations, staffing, and infrastructure. Donahoe wants to end Saturday delivery. He wants to consolidate what were once seven hundred mail processing facilities down to just two hundred. He wants to close thousands of underutilized post offices. He wants, through attrition, to cut another 155,500 jobs.

In 2012, seeking authorization to initiate his five-year "Plan to Profitability," Donahoe minced few words:

> Our business model is broken. We have insufficient revenue to cover our costs and are rapidly approaching our statutory debt limit of $15 billion. If the Postal Service were a private company, we would be engaged in Chapter 11 bankruptcy proceedings. Our financial crisis is the result of a restrictive business model and a permanent and fundamental shift away from First-Class Mail. During the past five years, the Postal Service recorded cumulative losses of $25 billion.

Congress, however, failed to pass any of the legislative relief the post office asked for, and in early 2013, Donahoe was back with more bad news. The Postal Service lost nearly $16 billion in 2012; indeed, it had experienced net losses for fourteen of the preceding sixteen quarters. It was losing some $25 million every day, and at one point in 2012 was less than four days away from running out of cash. Donahoe projected that without immediate and radical reform, the USPS's debt would balloon to $45 billion by 2017. "We are," the postmaster general said with epic understatement, "on an unsustainable path."

How did this happen? The short answer is that the very legal controls that protected the Postal Service for over two hundred years have, in the face of Big Bang Disruption, sealed its doom. The USPS, like that of most countries, has long operated as a regulated monopoly. With monopoly power comes protection from traditional competition, but also inflexibility and a loss of innovative drive.

When substitute products and services arrive in the form of better and cheaper exponential technology (here electronic mail, electronic bill pay, digital content), monopolies can't respond in time—or, in the case of the post office, without breaking longstanding logjams in Congress.

More damaging still, the Postal Service's legal obligation to accept and deliver mail to and from every American means that it can't simply exit markets just because consumers have abandoned them. It must maintain an enormous infrastructure of employees, facilities, and networks that have to be operated no matter how fast business drops off. Even if regulators eventually allow it to shrink, the overhang of pensions, health care benefits, and other lifetime costs remain.

At one time for better, but now for worse, the Postal Service isn't a private company. It needs permission to diversify into new and potentially profitable services. It needs permission to cut back services that can no longer sustain themselves. It needs permission, in short, to go out of business.

The carnage doesn't just affect the post office and the taxpayers who will ultimately be left to pay the bills. On its own, the USPS employs almost half a million people. Yet the overall supply chain—private trucking, sorting, distribution, postal retailers—totals some 7.5 million people, comprising an astonishing 7 percent of U.S. GDP. Many of the post office's contractors are even more constrained than the service itself. They have only one possible customer.

If the USPS can't find a way out of its downward spiral soon, it could take down a sizeable portion of the U.S. economy with it.

Welcome to life—such as it is—in Entropy, the cold and often lonely final stage of Big Bang Disruption.

In the big bang theory of the universe, entropy is only a theoretical possibility, the logical end of a process of slow decay, as the energy of the universe becomes so dissipated that no real activity is possible. In this hypothetical state, the laws of physics turn strange. Temperatures approach absolute zero. Black holes have sucked in all light and heat. Nothing moves.

Entropy is very real in Big Bang Disruption. By the end of the Big Crunch, customers have abandoned the old industry and migrated en masse to the new. Most incumbents leave the dying industry and its supply chain, taking with them whichever of their inventories, assets, and intellectual property have retained value in the new ecosystem and selling, as quickly as they can, those that do not. Some old enterprises find profitable homes in the new world; some pivot to other industries. Some, like Kodak and Hummer, simply disappear.

A few stragglers often remain, electing to serve a small but consolidated group of legacy customers who can't or won't adopt better and cheaper products, and who, for whatever reason, are content to remain with goods—pocket calendars, home telephones, cash registers—that are worse and more expensive, if only because they are more familiar.

Other incumbents trapped in the limbo of Entropy may not be so fortunate. Perhaps they were simply caught unprepared for a sudden change in the environment, forced into bankruptcy or other frozen states of corporate existence that left them unable to respond to the Big Crunch until it was over.

Or perhaps, as with the Postal Service, they are legally obliged to stay behind even as the customers migrate elsewhere, going through the motions of old industry behaviors in a kind of postapocalyptic zombie world. They burn through cash by maintaining networks and infrastructure built for enormous business volume that has slowed to a trickle, until they're finally given permission to transform into new enterprises that are once again relevant, or simply allowed to die a natural death.

Whatever the reason, companies that remain in Entropy often find they have become their own most dangerous competitor, dragging themselves deeper into inaction just as they need to apply their resources to achieve escape velocity. Customers and collaborators lose interest; share prices hover in the cellar as investors disappear; key talent jumps ship. Attracting new leadership with new ideas is difficult.

Whatever assets the holdouts have left may be unusable, or at least unusable in their current form. Their productive energy is often dissipated, too decayed to do any work.

There are those who thrive in Entropy, or at least who find ways to manage a profit. For the rest, there's still a chance to salvage remaining assets, and to make a delayed but lifesaving exit. The three rules for this stage have been applied successfully by enterprises large and small; sometimes by the also-ran competitors of those who were too big to survive the Big Crunch. They are:

Rule 10. *Escape Your Own Black Hole*—As the lone remaining incumbent, it may seem as if there's no more competition to worry about. But beware the deadly behavior of your older products and services once better and cheaper alternatives are readily available. Legacy costs, legacy customers, and legacy regulation make it harder, not easier, to compete.

Rule 11. *Become Someone Else's Components*—As humbling as the idea may sound, companies trapped in Entropy often find their best hope is to shut down retail business and transform into a supplier of parts and other resources for innovators in markets emerging elsewhere. When you're losing the war, in other words, become an arms merchant.

Rule 12. *Move to a New Singularity*—Co-opt the tools of the disruptors and their investors, and use them to relocate your remaining assets to a healthier ecosystem. Sponsoring hackathons, opening innovation centers for entrepreneurs, and excelling at corporate venture capital can often buy you the access and equity you need to catch up for lost time and missed opportunities in the early stages.

RULE 10. ESCAPE YOUR OWN BLACK HOLE

As old industry supply chains sunset in response to the complete and often sudden adoption of a Big Bang Disruptor, residual markets may persist. Following a wave of consolidation and bankruptcies as competitors exit by choice or by necessity, one incumbent often stays behind, servicing the needs of customers who still want the older technology, even when better and cheaper alternatives exist. But often just one.

Only a fraction of the old revenue is available, but serving the remaining customers may still be profitable for a scaled-down enterprise that wants to try. The legacy customers may be older, with no particular need or incentives to switch to newer technologies that may, for them at least, pose a steep learning curve. Or they may be sentimentalists, who buy or keep the old products out of a sense of nostalgia—a word whose origin translates roughly as "painful homecoming."

In Chapter Three, we mentioned the rapid roll-up of manufacturers in the collapsing pinball industry of the 1990s, which left only Stern Pinball still making new games. Stern survived by selling machines to the few remaining arcades that wanted them. Later, it discovered a healthy new market selling arcade machines to aging baby boomers for home use. In 2012, Stern earned $50 million, a 33 percent increase from the previous year. "We are the only manufacturer of pinball machines in the world," CEO Gary Stern said in a 2013 interview. "We stick with it."

We also said earlier that Big Bang market adoption collapsed the five segments identified by Everett Rogers down to just two: trial users, and everybody else. Legacy customers represent a minor third category—a small but often devoted following that keeps old products alive and sustains the surviving incumbent long after disruptive technologies have deconstructed the old industry.

Such customers may seem like life preservers, but be wary—their continued devotion may become a kind of siren song, luring you ever closer to an inescapable black hole of increasing costs and declining revenues.

For one thing, serving legacy customers requires the surviving incumbent to take on the duties of every departed participant in its supply chain, building, distributing, and servicing products built on now-inferior technologies. Servicing legacy customers may require the same fleet of vehicles and technicians, warehouses of replacement parts that may be harder and more expensive to maintain, and call centers originally built to support a growing business. While participants in the new ecosystem can lease flexible, cloud-based information systems, incumbents often find themselves stuck maintaining increasingly brittle legacy software and aging technology infrastructure whose high costs they may still be amortizing.

What were once economies of scale, in the reversed physics of Entropy, become diseconomies. That's because fixed costs don't scale down. Neither do pension obligations, retiree health care benefits, or unexpired warranties. They hang over your head, threatening doom.

The costs and logistics of maintaining obsolete technologies is an enormous headache for providers and customers alike, especially in rapidly changing consumer electronics and computing markets. Leading software companies including Microsoft, Adobe, Google, and Intuit spend heavily to support products they are no longer actively marketing, hoping the investment pays off by easing users into current and next-generation replacements.

Dropping support when a product loses popularity is often too dangerous an alternative to contemplate. Consider Sony's 2007 decision to abandon its proprietary ATRAC standard, a file format the company imposed on customers who purchased digital music for use with Sony audio players.

Not only were users required to convert their prior purchases,

Sony actually advised them to do so by burning their ATRAC files to a disc and then converting them to another format. That was the only way around digital locks Sony had put in place to protect itself from piracy—a likely contributor to the market's unenthusiastic response to the ATRAC standard in the first place. The company's mishandling of ATRAC's termination set Sony's digital strategy back by a decade.

Motorola likewise raised the hackles of customers of its Photon 4G smartphone. When launching the device in 2011, Motorola promised to keep it up to date with new releases of the Android operating system for at least eighteen months. Twelve months later, however, Motorola reneged on that pledge, and did so in a post buried in an obscure corner of its online user forum. Though Motorola offered a $100 credit to disappointed Photon buyers, many customers swore off the company's future products for good.

When exit isn't an option, the best a surviving incumbent can hope for is to carefully manage a small market. Even the small market may continue to shrink, as legacy customers migrate, albeit begrudgingly, to Big Bang alternatives. The remaining users may also be older, and aging. At some point they will no longer need your products, or any products at all.

Finding new customers for goods and services associated with a receding past is a daunting prospect. Some car companies, including Cadillac, have made significant headway migrating from older to younger car buyers. Newspapers, at least in their paper form, have not. Daily circulation in the United States has declined over 20 percent in the last decade, while advertising revenue, adjusted for inflation, has dropped to 1950 levels.

For newspapers, the demographic trends are even more ominous. According to a 2012 Pew Research Center survey, only 16 percent of respondents between ages forty and forty-nine say they read a newspaper the previous day, a number that fell to 6 percent for those between eighteen and twenty-four. (See Figure 24.) Even if

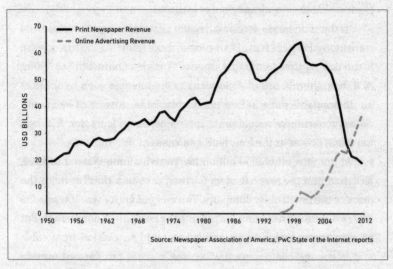

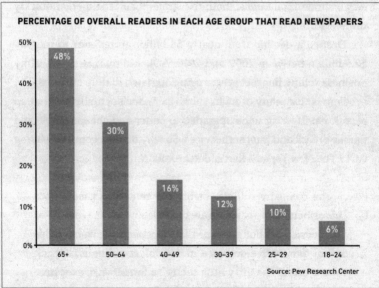

FIGURE 24. The Disappearance of Printed Newspapers

newspapers keep all of their remaining readers, from an actuarial perspective they're already out of business.

In the worst-case scenario, legacy customers may have already transitioned to a Big Bang Disruptor without knowing it. That, at least, is the ticking time bomb that worries America Online. In the 1990s, AOL brought millions of Americans to the Internet, seen by some as an unstoppable force in Internet access. Legal advocates even petitioned government regulators to intervene, out of fears that AOL had too much power as the Internet's gatekeeper.

At the time of its $350 billion merger with Time Warner in 2000, AOL had half the revenue of its partner, yet was valued at twice the price of the much older company. The merged entity was intended to marry access with content, increasing the company's dominance. But as new access technologies arrived in rapid succession from cable and telephone companies, and as free content proliferated outside AOL's curated "channels," both the strategy and the merger quickly unraveled.

Despite a decline from nearly $8 billion in revenue to roughly $2.5 billion between 2000 and 2010, AOL still maintains a healthy business selling Internet access using outdated dial-up modems. The problem is that many of AOL's subscribers don't actually use dial-up access, having long since upgraded to better and cheaper cable and mobile broadband Internet services. So why do they continue paying AOL? The *New Yorker*'s Ken Auletta explains:

> The company still gets eighty per cent of its profits from subscribers, many of whom are older people who have cable or DSL service but don't realize that they need not pay an additional twenty-five dollars a month to get online and check their e-mail. "The dirty little secret," a former AOL executive says, "is that seventy-five per cent of the people who subscribe to AOL's dial-up service don't need it."

Eventually, of course, those subscriptions will expire, either because the children of AOL's aging users will explain it to them or because the customers themselves will, well, expire. If the company doesn't find some other source of revenue by then, it may join its remaining customers in the great beyond.

Sometimes even incumbents with both the ways and the means to escape are nonetheless trapped in Entropy, less by legacy customers than by legacy regulations. In public utilities, as the example of the USPS suggests, the collapsing gravity of a black hole may be generated by legal requirements and rules that prohibit market exit and enforce quality-of-service requirements and open-access demands.

These sorts of protections are invariably imposed when the provider operated as a regulated monopoly, with no possibility of competitors who could impose market discipline. The restrictions, in economic terms, are necessary evils to ensure essential services are available to everyone.

But as customers migrate to better and cheaper alternatives that are free of regulation, the added gravitational pressure on incumbents who must continue to operate as utilities can quickly grow unbearable. You can't beat better and cheaper with worse and more expensive, especially when worse and more expensive has to stay that way as a matter of law.

That's the crisis now facing incumbent landline telephone companies including, in the United States, Verizon and AT&T. Once part of the regulated Bell monopoly, the two companies continue to offer old-fashioned switched telephone connections, or what is known as Plain Old Telephone Service (POTS), under heavy regulatory constraints from a variety of federal, state, and local government agencies. Pricing, quality, and access to facilities by competitors are all regulated on the slow and inefficient clock speed of ponderous government agencies.

Landline customers, meanwhile, are accelerating their move to exponential communications technologies, including cable, fiber, and high-speed mobile communications. In the United States and elsewhere, voice customers have abandoned wired telephone service in favor of Internet telephony, or Voice Over IP, at a remarkable rate. As recently as a decade ago, POTS connected nearly every American. Yet by the end of 2011, less than half of U.S. homes still had a wired connection. That number could fall to 25 percent by 2015.

While phone companies once dismissed the Internet as a potentially better telephone network, carriers large and small have since embraced IP as the only option to satisfy the exploding demand of mobile technology users, cloud-based services, and the coming data deluge of "machine to machine" communications. Improvements to digital networks, as we have seen, follow the curve of exponential technologies. The Internet's design, moreover, doesn't really care if the packets it transmits contain voice, data, or video content. As Nicholas Negroponte famously said in 1999, "Bits are bits."

The Internet's combination of better and cheaper networks and flexible design has opened an enormous black hole for POTS carriers. As customers abandon landline services and equipment suppliers consolidate, the cost of maintaining aging copper and analog switches is rising dramatically, both in absolute terms and on a per-customer basis. The operating expense for a native IP network can be as much as 90 percent less than for POTS. Legacy carriers spend as much as 50 percent of their budget keeping old networks running for fewer users.

To their credit, the incumbent providers are racing to retire and replace what had been, until recently, their most valuable assets. Both Verizon and AT&T have spent billions accelerating the replacement of copper with fiber, and circuit-switched equipment with packet-switched equipment. The legacy carriers have invested even more in building mobile broadband networks—the Big Bang Disruptor that is nipping at the heels of even broadband wired services.

Still, legacy carriers can't simply turn off the old POTS network, despite their progress in replacing it with something better and cheaper. By law, telephone network operators cannot retire the POTS network without federal and perhaps state regulatory permission, even if superior alternatives are in place. And the FCC has balked at giving permission for the switchover, in part because state regulators and local telephone companies that still use the incumbent's analog equipment to offer competing local phone service each worry about losing their relevance.

The longer the carriers are required to spend money maintaining the obsolete networks, the less capital budget is available to speed up the replacement of that equipment with better and cheaper IP technologies, including fiber optics, digital switches, and upgrades to straining cellular networks.

In the end, the real victims of the regulatory logjam are the remaining landline users who are also, not surprisingly, the customers least likely to be taking advantage of any Internet services. Rural residents, seniors, and low-income families are furthest behind in broadband adoption, according to government data. They are also the groups with the highest percentages of users still relying on switched telephone networks as their only form of communication.

Getting these communities onto IP networks sooner rather than later would eliminate the need for expensive maintenance of the obsolete switched infrastructure. It would also make it easier and less expensive for them to connect to other broadband services including video and Internet access, fast becoming necessities for jobs, education, entertainment, health care, and public safety.

In that sense, allowing the carriers to accelerate the transition to digital networks, as they have repeatedly petitioned the government for permission to do, would significantly counter the obstacles that keep 20 percent of American adults from joining the Internet. According to the Pew Internet Project, almost half of them cite a lack of relevance to their needs, rather than cost, as their primary reason not to connect. With the switch to Internet telephone service, demonstrating the clear value of other Internet services would prove that much easier to accomplish.

For now, there doesn't seem to be enough regulatory urgency to save the legacy customers who most need help, or the carriers who are trying to do the right thing. This is an ironic reversal of laws that were enacted to ensure equal access to new technologies for all communities.

RULE 11. BECOME SOMEONE ELSE'S COMPONENTS

If you do find yourself in Entropy, achieving escape velocity is hard. You may be held back by legacy customers, or even legacy regulators who genuinely want to support you, but wind up pulling you deeper into a black hole. They may encourage or even require you to maintain the infrastructure and supply chain of a dying technology. As customer populations dwindle, diseconomies of scale will make competing with better and cheaper Big Bang Disruptors even harder.

A more promising approach is to embrace the void, at least for aspects of your business that simply can't be salvaged. Allow products to sunset, and terminate ongoing financial obligations including warranties and pension benefits as soon as it is legal and responsible to do so. Let intellectual property with no residual value go with them.

In other words, dismantle your existing balance sheet before forces outside your control do it for you. Then take what is left and find uses for it in other industries and other ecosystems. Instead of continuing to sell products that have fewer buyers, become someone else's components, available for new innovation and, potentially, new Big Bang Disruptors.

Going from producer to supplier will require some creative

rebranding for both your enterprise and your assets. Much of your existing infrastructure—including retail and distribution networks and human resources—will not survive the transition. A long and distinguished corporate history may open onto a modest new chapter. Still, many seemingly obsolete companies have managed it, breathing new life into old ideas and finding uses for them in other products.

In the end, you may only salvage one product. But one product could be enough to make you more profitable than ever.

That's what happened to Texas Instruments. The company, now celebrating more than seventy-five years in the electronics industries, is a global behemoth with annual revenue of more than $12.8 billion. Credited with inventing the integrated circuit, TI is the third largest manufacturer of semiconductors in the world and the second largest supplier of chips for cell phones. It is an essential provider of component parts to industries as varied as education, medicine, security, telecommunications, and electronics.

Yet the company nearly fell victim to a Big Crunch.

In the 1970s, TI was a very different business than it is today. At that time, in addition to semiconductors, it sold a wide range of consumer electronics under its own brand, including digital clocks, LED wristwatches, and high-end scientific calculators.

In 1979 the company expanded into what was then the most exciting market there was: home computers. This was a new market, distinct from business computers, with offerings that were far more affordable and targeted directly at early adopters and hobbyists. The TI-99/4A, launched in 1981, was a great success. It was the first 16-bit personal computer, offering advanced voice-synthesis capabilities and plug-and-play peripherals. It is still venerated by its one-time users.

Throughout the early 1980s, TI held a significant share of the home computer market. But a withering price war with rivals, including Osborne and Commodore, pressured the company to begin selling its home computers at an untenably low price. By 1983, the TI-99/4A, unveiled with a list price of over $500, had dropped to only $150.

The home-computer market, at least temporarily, was saturated. And TI was left with an unsustainable investment that quickly pulled the other 90 percent of the company—made up mostly of semiconductors and military applications—to the edge of solvency. TI abruptly pulled out. After selling nearly three million home computers, the company ended the business with losses estimated at $500 million.

TI was saved by a toy. More specifically, by a single part inside a toy.

In the late 1970s, TI had launched a series of educational products, including the Speak & Spell, which helped teach children the basics of language and math. In a typical application, the device verbalized a list of words and then invited the child, using a small keyboard, to spell them. Built to leverage TI's expertise in voice synthesis, the Speak & Spell had interchangeable game cartridges and was perhaps the first extendable home gaming device. It was a hit for the company, selling in various incarnations until 1992.

The Speak & Spell represented the first commercial use of digital signal processing technology, or DSP. DSPs are tiny silicon workhorses optimized to take digital signals including audio and video and analyze them in real time using mathematically intensive algorithms. Since their introduction in 1979, DSPs have powered applications from amplifiers to voice recognition systems.

Today, they are critical components in many exponential technologies, including smart phones, robotics, and automobile safety systems like antilock brakes. DSPs are now found in radar and sonar systems, and in medical equipment including MRIs, CT scanners, and ultrasounds.

After closing its home computer business, TI quickly reinvented itself as a supplier of DSPs to other manufacturers. Since 1980, TI has been the world's leader in DSP production, which represents about $1.97 billion of the company's annual revenue. By 2008, TI controlled 65 percent of the DSP market worldwide. Though the company's focus later shifted to analog components, a significant portion of TI's business is still dedicated to signal processing.

With the sunsetting of one business, TI found a way to leverage one of its assets to create a new one, taking on the role of supplier. Instead of selling directly to consumers, TI nurtured a community of DSP programmers and algorithm designers, who in turn discovered new uses for the company's products. DSPs are now being used as math coprocessors for supercomputers, for example, taking the products into the realm of weather prediction, financial analysis, and computer vision.

"TI became the first company with a sophisticated signal-processing chip and also understood that the device was not the product," DSP pioneer and TI Principal Fellow Gene Frantz said in a 2012 interview. "The product was the device plus support plus the development environment plus a device hotline. We created a product for customers to use in their product."

TI's experience of rapid decline taught the company an important lesson in this last stage of Big Bang Disruption. When all seems lost, it may only be the last version of your product that customers are abandoning. The underlying technologies that fueled that product can find new users and new markets—markets that may prove more valuable now than before the fall.

From being a frontline combatant in a home PC market that practiced mutually assured destruction, TI created a DSP business, transforming into an arms merchant to competitors in a different war. That shift required not so much discovering a new technology as accepting a new role in a different ecosystem. That's a change that can be humbling for onetime market leaders. But for TI, reinvention came with minimal trauma, a legacy perhaps of the company's long-standing involvement in exponential products.

Pivoting away from your own declining markets to become a component supplier may be too traumatic a cultural shift to stomach for companies that dominate their industry. Yet it is often a winning strategy for second- and third-place competitors, giving them the final victory that may have eluded them in earlier markets. In Chapter Six, we noted the failure of photo processing giant Kodak. As we saw, when a gradual decline in chemical-based imaging became sudden with the smartphone revolution, Kodak fell into bankruptcy, barely selling its residual intellectual property in time.

Compare that experience to the parallel story of Fujifilm, Kodak's longtime Japanese competitor. Unlike Kodak, Fujifilm managed to repurpose its expertise and technology to adjacent industries and markets, squeezing that much more value from the sunsetting photography business. High-definition imaging, for example, has translated into entry into the nascent nanotechnology field. The company has also entered the pharmaceutical business, looking at ways to improve the absorption of chemicals in drugs, including flu vaccines.

Fujifilm also leveraged its expertise in antioxidation technology into—of all places—cosmetics. Here, technology perfected by Fujifilm to prevent photographs from fading caused by ultraviolet radiation has been adapted to do the same for human skin. In both cases, oxidation disintegrates collagen, an element common to both film and skin. Fujifilm already knew how to create emulsions that protected against oxidation on film, technology now at the heart of its Astalift skincare products.

In some sense, Fujifilm has its old rival to thank for a culture that encouraged diversification into unrelated markets. To achieve the scale Fujifilm needed to compete with Kodak in the film business, Fujifilm needed to find uses for its products in other markets. In the late 1990s, for example, the company turned its ability to produce ultrathin layers of photographic film to the nascent flat-screen-display market. That move has given Fujifilm control of roughly 80 percent of the global market for protective film for LCD televisions.

When the end finally came for film photography, Fujifilm had the skills and organizationally flexibility to move quickly. "Technologically, we already possessed diverse resources," the company's chief executive Shigetaka Komori told the *Wall Street Journal* in 2012. "So we thought, 'There must be ways to turn them into new businesses.'"

Which is exactly what he did. In 2004, Komori, who had become chief executive the year before, announced a "second inauguration" for the company, one that would reduce its reliance on photographic film from 20 percent to only 1 percent over the next decade. At the same time, the company's move into health care grew to over 10 percent of Fujifilm's annual $22 billion in revenue. The LCD business generates another 10 percent.

That kind of resurrection is hardly easy. In the post-film world, Komori has been forced to make wrenching sacrifices, cutting billions in costs and shedding thousands of jobs. The wind down of the photography business cost the company some $2.5 billion. When the global financial crisis hit, Komori cut another $2 billion.

Still, the results speak for themselves. In 2012, as Kodak was declaring bankruptcy, Fujifilm was valued at over $12 billion. The company had escaped its dying industry.

RULE 12. MOVE TO A NEW SINGULARITY

The final strategy for escaping Entropy is the boldest of them all: find a Big Bang market still in the early stage of failed market experimentation, and then reconfigure your business to become part of its emerging ecosystem. Take your brand and your intellectual property, in other words, and move to a new Singularity.

Depending on your stomach for change and the remaining assets you bring, your role in any new Singularity will vary. Our research suggests, however, that the most successful companies to implement this strategy adopt a three-step approach:

1. First, they *reach out* to early stage entrepreneurs as collaborators, trading established brand and expertise for access to new thinking from those at the leading edge of technological change.
2. Once they find promising developers and technologies, they *bring the entrepreneurs inside*, offering them infrastructure and other resources in well-appointed innovation labs located in key technology hubs.
3. Finally, for the most promising disruptors, they *invest directly*, often alongside traditional venture capitalists, gaining both potential upside and early access to new disruptors.

We have already mentioned one emerging best practice for collaborating with experimenters in a new Singularity. In Chapter Four, recall, we described our experience serving as judges in a San Francisco hackathon that developed dozens of prototypes for smartphone apps focused on helping adults and children with autism and their families and other caregivers.

That hackathon was cosponsored by the AT&T Developer's Program and Autism Speaks, a national advocacy group. The event was just one of nearly monthly hackathons, part of an elaborate program of outreach intended to raise the profile of AT&T's mobile networking technology.

The AT&T Developer's Program, a creation of the company's senior executive vice president of technology John Donovan, holds regular events, and not just in Silicon Valley. In 2013, the company sponsored hackathons in emerging technology hubs including New York, Chicago, Austin, Miami, and Tel Aviv.

Some of these events are focused on particular mobile technologies, while others address specific application needs. All of them, however, give developers free access to AT&T technology resources, interfaces, and development experts. On the other side of the equation, the hackathons give AT&T access to the latest thinking in how mobile devices are being included in new Big Bang Disruptors.

AT&T's goal, of course, is to get the best new products launched first on its wireless network. In the mobile ecosystem, as we've already seen, consumers care less about network design than they do about the latest device, operating system, and, most of all, the apps. So the Developer's Program is tasked with getting the best and most diverse apps working with the networks and equipment of AT&T and its partners, including Ericsson, Cisco, Intel, and Microsoft. Together, these companies have invested over $100 million in developer outreach efforts.

AT&T is hardly alone in embracing hackathons as a tool to give incumbents access to the leading edge of technology experiments. As more industries come under the gravitational pull of exponential technologies and the disruptive power of near-perfect market information, more executives are looking to construct whatever early warning systems they can. Hackathons, which quickly and cheaply unearth interesting technologies, applications, and entrepreneurs, can provide impressive payback.

As we've seen, hackathons can also test a new product idea in a matter of days or even hours. So it's little surprise to find these events taking place every day and across the globe. In recent months, we've seen hackathons organized by enterprises as varied as newspaper chains, cancer research foundations, and city governments. Everyone, it seems, wants to tap into the power of combinatorial innovation to break out of old patterns and escape the icy grip of Entropy.

A recent event at the University of Michigan, for example, drew teams from more than two dozen different universities, producing 125 hacks. Prize money was provided by a who's who of technology companies and venture investors, including Facebook, Google, Groupon, Barracuda Networks, and Andreessen Horowitz, the investment firm started by Internet pioneer Marc Andreessen.

When outreach programs unearth promising projects and talent, the second step is to nurture their development into market experiments. To accelerate that process, many incumbents have created innovation centers. The innovation center can be a kind of permanent and intensive hackathon, where developers are given working space, hardware and software, and more direct access to the incumbent's technology and expertise.

AT&T, for example, has opened centers it calls "Foundries" in Silicon Valley, Texas, and Israel, where promising projects are brought in-house and given full-time resources to help bring them to market. One example is SundaySky, a video publishing environment. Its developers were invited to take up residence after a "fast pitch" session, where developers get just a few minutes to describe their projects. Less than five months later, AT&T's U-verse video service conducted a trial using the SundaySky technology to provide customers with personalized, interactive video "bills."

At Accenture, our global Capital Markets industry group has long been a sponsor and active participant of the FinTech Innovation Labs in New York and London, an incubator that admits six companies yearly into a twelve-week program providing mentoring, access to industry leaders, and work space in Manhattan.

FinTech focuses on new technologies for the financial services industry. According to Bob Gach, Accenture's managing director for Capital Markets, "Banks have a growing appetite for external solutions driven by their efforts to reduce costs, a tight investment cycle, and a need for commercial solutions that they might have developed with their own investments before."

Innovation centers and industry-focused incubators are a new variation on the kind of early stage nurturing that has long been instrumental in taking disruptive technologies from basic research to commercial applications. While early incubators were often built and operated by research universities, over the last twenty years incubation has been successfully adapted by incumbents and others looking to connect entrepreneurs to the company's existing technology resources.

In addition to getting the best thinking of new talent, innovation centers help the incumbents discover the true value of their own technology. They also help overcome cultural or legal obstacles that make it difficult for incumbents to reinvent themselves using internal resources.

In most innovation centers, the exchange between established industry participants and entrepreneurs is informational rather than financial. The developers who take up temporary residence own the resulting products and services outright, or may enter into ownership-sharing agreements with the incubator's sponsors, funders, or some combination.

For the most promising experiments, or for those that require more dedicated resources, collaboration with entrepreneurs often leads to the third step in the move to a new Singularity: acquiring a financial stake in start-ups.

Investment by incumbents in early market experiments, known as corporate venture capital (CVC), also has a long history. In the late 1990s, during the dot-com boom, it seemed that every company was creating a CVC fund, hoping to cash in on the irrational exuberance of early Internet IPOs. When the public markets returned to firmer ground, many of these funds were terminated and the CVC operations shut down.

In the age of Big Bang Disruption, CVC has returned, smarter and more focused. Today's corporate investors are not simply trying to make fast money. Instead, they are using capital markets to gain awareness and access to technologies with the potential to disrupt their own businesses. Their strategy is to find the most promising early market experiments and invest in them before those efforts achieve catastrophic success.

Venture capitalists and entrepreneurs, at the same time, value CVC partners as more than just junior investors. Incumbents also offer highly motivated internal users, market expertise, and, potentially, a future channel partner for finished products and services.

In the last few years, companies including Google, KT Corp, and China's Tencent have committed billions to venture investing, making them major players in the intricate capital markets that fuel new Singularities. CVC has become a driving force in a variety of technology and data-intensive industries, including energy, transportation, financial services, and manufacturing.

In the growing "clean" energy sector, for example, more than 20 percent of venture investments today include a corporate partner. Companies investing in green technology include oil giant Shell, as well as transportation companies such as General Motors and BMW.

According to trade publication *Global Corporate Venturing*, more than two hundred companies around the world created or relaunched CVC operations between 2010 and 2013. There are more than one thousand active corporate venturing funds and units, which invested in more than one thousand deals worth more than $18 billion in 2013, of which the United States accounts for about two-thirds. The numbers are still growing.

Getting it right requires a mix of old and new skills. In our work with CVC expert Heidi Mason, managing partner of the Bell Mason Group and coauthor of *The Venture Imperative*, we've seen how CVC efforts succeed only when led by investment professionals who have the ability to work closely with senior management and business leaders inside the sponsoring company.

CVC programs must also commit to long-term collaboration with portfolio companies and the venture community. Successful corporate investors live and work among the traditional investors and entrepreneurs, fostering the kind of informal relationships and cultural cross-pollination that is essential to survive in the fast-paced world of a new Singularity.

CVC units typically invest alongside traditional venture capital funds. That means that the fund's managers must excel at core skills of early stage investment, including deal flow, portfolio management, and active board-level support for portfolio companies. Fund managers need the authority to respond quickly to investment opportunities that may be otherwise snatched up by others.

Successful CVC units also require a second kind of expertise. Inside the parent organization, an office of venturing, led by the chief innovation officer, must coordinate the company's full portfolio of future-looking investments, including CVC, traditional research and development, joint ventures and acquisitions, and internally incubated projects.

There is also a new emphasis on integrating CVC activities with the parent company's overall innovation agenda, connecting CVC with formerly separate efforts at incubation and research and development. "CVC is part of the execution," Mason says, "but the catalyst comes from the company's innovation and growth strategy. And that is the responsibility of senior management, coordinated by the chief innovation officer." With awareness of a company's entire innovation portfolio, management can avoid being blindsided by Big Bang Disruption.

To help CVC fund managers focus their portfolio on technologies most likely to disrupt the core business, each investment must also be paired with an internal corporate sponsor who works closely with the start-up. The business partner provides complementary technology and industry expertise. More valuable still, it commits to being an early user of the portfolio company's products.

In the new CVC model, investment performance is measured not only by return on capital but also return on the intangibles.

Investments must generate not only financial returns, in other words, but also strategic returns. Did the investment filter back into the investing organization, for example, helping it better understand emerging technologies? Did the investment gain the company experience and contacts in emerging global markets? Did the investment expand the company's exposure to outside innovators, investors, and their customers? Did it lead to the development of new products and services with significant potential to move the investing company into new businesses?

These are the kinds of questions driving successful CVC efforts at financial juggernaut Citigroup. On the brink of the recent crisis in financial services in 2008, Citi's then-new CEO Vikram Pandit appointed the company's first chief innovation officer, Deborah Hopkins. "Our CEO was told that the company had lost its ability to innovate," Hopkins told us. "He told us to get it back."

Hopkins initial work involved experiments in Asia, where guerilla teams designed and tested prototype retail storefronts that catered to the needs of busy, on-the-go consumers. That led to a project in Japan, where Citi worked with the designers of Apple's retail stores, Eight Inc., to create Smart Banking, an initiative that reduced 156 processes down to just 12 and then built branches that optimized the customer experience around them. To date, over 130 Smart Banking branches have been opened in Asia. Global expansion of the model is well under way.

During a 2009 visit to Silicon Valley, however, Hopkins realized that the only way to get access to leading-edge technologies of critical importance to Citi's future was to invest in them. And that meant taking up residence. Hopkins sold her Manhattan home and moved to Palo Alto, where she has since built Citi Ventures, a team of twenty professionals, including satellites in New York and Shanghai.

As any VC will tell you, a full-time on-the-ground presence is a necessary condition for successful CVC co-investing. Relocating its first chief innovation officer, on the other hand, sent an undeniable signal that Citi was serious about disruptive innovation.

The bank's investment philosophy emphasizes access to game-changing entrepreneurs. According to its charter, Citi Ventures invests to "leverage the power of social media and information analytics, facilitate continuous mobility, increase security and prevent fraud, and introduce new forms of digital goods and services." Hopkins is looking for nothing less than those innovations with the potential to reinvent Citi's core business with new technologies and business models that create unique, fresh customer experiences.

Citi also brings more to the table than just investment dollars. "We stay with the company every step of the way. We want to be the champion of the start-up," Hopkins said. That means working with portfolio companies to navigate the bank's various businesses and vast geographic footprint, ensuring that the start-up's technology has its best opportunity to be tested and adopted inside of Citi. "Our IT organization does an amazing job helping these companies scale their offerings to effectively process the massive volumes Citi manages. Being able to say Citi has deployed their product is worth more than the money we invest," Hopkins notes. "It puts them on the map."

One of the first investments, a security start-up called Silver Tail Systems, exemplifies both the hard work and good luck that distinguishes Citi's successful CVC efforts. Hopkins first heard about the company during a meeting with Andreessen Horowitz. Silver Tail's technology, which uses sophisticated analysis of a Web site user's navigation to quickly spot behavior that signals attempted security breaches, immediately got her attention. After meeting with the start-up's two founders, Hopkins's instincts told her they had made a profound breakthrough.

Hopkins and her team had to move fast—and did. Andreessen Horowitz was about to close on financing for Silver Tail, but Hopkins was able to get approval to invest in only a few weeks. From there,

Hopkins made introductions to Citi's IT leadership, who shared her enthusiasm. Within eight weeks, the company had already started a pilot of Silver Tail's product.

The results of the pilot were immediate and impressive. The software, Hopkins says, demonstrated "unprecedented capability to identify security threats and fraudulent behavior patterns." Within months, Silver Tail had signed a contract with Citi, and soon after, with other large banks.

"Having Citi as an investor was nothing like the traditional venture capitalists we had worked with in the past," according to Laura Mather, PhD, founder and chief visionary of Silver Tail. "The value they brought in getting us to the right people within Citi, making sure the typical hurdles were cleared expediently, and then telling others—both banks and press—about our success within the bank was nothing short of game changing for us."

Less than eighteen months after Hopkins first heard of the company, Silver Tail was acquired for an undisclosed price by EMC. On top of everything else, that meant a nice return for Citi on its financial—as well as its strategic—investment.

The bank has even higher ambitions for Citi Ventures. Its investment activity has become a potent source of truth-telling about the future of financial services and the changing needs of its ultra-connected, technology-obsessed clients and customers.

"We might look at eight hundred companies and invest in only five," Hopkins says. "But in reality we're building domain knowledge through those meetings, and translating it into best practices and benchmarks we can share with our worldwide organization."

In that sense, CVC isn't just a hedge against the growing threat of disruptions assailing companies from every corner. For incumbents like Citi, it's a first-class ticket to new innovations and new growth. And to Big Bang Disruptors of their own.

Incumbents that have embraced corporate venture capital, hackathons, and innovation centers are the new pioneers, breaking out of Entropy and finding new Singularities while there is still time and resources to reinvent themselves. These companies don't live in denial of the powerful potential of emerging technologies. Nor do they bemoan the tendency of such disruptions to visit chaos on their industries. Instead, they have discovered mutually beneficial ways of working with start-ups and the technologies they bring with them, and of applying that skill early and often.

From the beginning of the shark fin to its end, effective partnering is critical. Success at Big Bang Disruption is always a function of your ability to work well within an ecosystem. Rigid strategies and heavy-handed dealings with longtime supply chain partners must give way to experimentation and collaboration. A closed corporate culture has become a liability; openness to new ideas and new partners has become an invaluable and crucial asset.

An emphasis on openness and collaboration may seem paradoxical in an environment where a second place finish is often unprofitable. But to capture winner-take-all markets, you must first disabuse yourself of the idea that you are already, by virtue of what might be a long history of success, entitled to them. In creating Big Bang Disruptors, humility, not arrogance, is the true measure of confidence.

That confidence is essential—without it, you won't be prepared when near-perfect market information transforms your experiments into breakthrough products and services. Catastrophic success becomes, without an ecosystem to back you up, just plain catastrophe.

In Big Bang Disruption, time is always the most critical resource. In our survey of disruptions old and new, perfect timing—whether to launch an experiment, acquire a start-up, scale up or scale down production, sell an asset, or liquidate an inventory—separates every billion-dollar success from every billion-dollar bankruptcy.

Perfect timing only looks like a function of exceptionally good luck. It is in fact a hard-earned skill. It requires the wisdom to find and interpret the messages of truth-tellers, and the intellectual and computing horsepower to crunch all the big data you can get your hands on. For master clock makers, it means slowing the world down to bullet time and pinpointing the moment of saturation long before it happens.

We've come to the end of the Big Bang life cycle, or rather, to one turn of it. Time for a few closing thoughts and directions for future study. And before you know it, another round of exponential technologies and another Singularity in which to experiment with them.

CONCLUSION

As the story of Citi Ventures underscores, there's hope for incumbents at every stage of Big Bang Disruption, even when their industries are facing their darkest hours and most severe crises. The imminent devastation of today's business may be just the motivation you need to discover the true value of your assets, and inspire you to achieve your full potential as an innovator. Like Twitter, Starbucks, and Airbnb, Citi learned the lessons of disruptive innovation, if for no other reason than because it had to.

But there is no guarantee that the twelve rules of Big Bang Disruption will save anybody. Whether you are an incumbent or a start-up, your survival depends critically on the commitment and wisdom of senior management. Ultimately, success in Big Bang Disruption requires leaders who can navigate out of the desert of abandoned products and markets to find new ways of building and launching disruptive goods and services. It's not enough just to send out the scouts and wait.

Other leadership skills are equally important. Strategy in the age of devastating innovation demands an abundance of courage throughout the shark fin. Danger lurks at every stage. From the market, incumbents face the threat of better and cheaper products and services, many of which don't appear on the competitive radar until it's too late. From the boardroom, the essential transformation of the business is constantly beset by the organization's natural immune response, fine-tuned to resist any change—even those essential to the survival of the enterprise.

To avoid these obstacles, leaders must be brutally honest about the changing dynamics of their industries and the declining value of their remaining resources. As assets morph into liabilities with alarming speed, senior executives must keep a constant vigil over the balance sheet, reassessing the true value of existing brands, inventories, physical plant and intellectual property, free of distracting sentimentality.

For those who can make a break with the past, there is cause for optimism. Rapidly falling transaction costs freed many of the companies in our study from the shackles of unwieldy supply chains. Liberated from depleted assets and crushing inventories, they discovered new roles to play in the next incarnation of their industries, or in adjacent industries where just a few of their old skills proved valuable—perhaps extremely so—to new customers and partners.

Companies such as Texas Instruments and Fujifilm overcame the shocking disappearance of profitable customers and the sudden obsolescence of core technologies. Kodak, Fujifilm's longtime rival, did not. Despite pleas to regulators for permission to evolve, the United States Postal Service, at least so far, has not been allowed to respond to existential changes to its business, and may soon require an act of Congress to avoid further debt.

The role that incumbents play in emerging Big Bang ecosystems will certainly be different from today. What will you change into? Our research suggests that successful businesses choose from among four new kinds of specialization, equally available to entrepreneurs and large enterprises:

- *Inventors—Researchers that create better and cheaper technologies.* Inventors provide scientific advancement, often through exponential improvement in key components or raw inputs and materials. They also provide production process breakthroughs that dramatically lower the cost of manufacturing. One great example is Corning, whose engineers accidentally created the core technology of Gorilla Glass only to rediscover it years later to create a breakthrough product when new uses appeared. Companies pursuing new battery technologies for everything from cars to cell phones are another example.

- *Designers—Specialists in combining off-the-shelf component parts to create new products and services.* Designers excel at creating compelling products using the technologies of inventors. They differentiate their products with superior user interfaces and other features that generate fanatic followings (and invaluable brand awareness) among dedicated customers. Apple has been a longtime design specialist, most recently with its consumer electronics and mobile devices such as the iPhone and iPad, assembled largely from off-the-shelf parts. Even Twitter, recall, was born of a simple experiment that combined existing technologies in a new configuration—just to see what would happen.

- *Producers—Experts in providing component parts for ecosystems where demand can rise and fall dramatically and suddenly.* Producers provide high-volume, high-speed manufacturing and distribution of key raw materials for use by designers, offsetting their risk of making too little or too much of their Big Bang Disruptors. Texas Instruments, as we saw, transformed itself from a company that made electronic goods sold under its own name to a provider of core technology parts for other companies.

- *Assemblers—Process experts who use the designs and parts of others to manufacture finished goods on demand.* Assemblers combine primarily off-the-shelf parts to create products and services on behalf of designers. They specialize in responding efficiently to volatile demand and are able to scale up and scale down without sacrificing cost and efficiency. Foxconn, which assembles many of the consumer electronic goods of Apple and other designers, is a good example of this new breed of outsourcer. Assemblers can also include services, such as Airbnb and Uber, that bring together consumers and suppliers, respectively, of rentable rooms and rides, building "products" on a transaction-by-transaction basis.

Although our research on specialization within Big Bang ecosystems is still in progress, a few insights have already emerged. The first is that specialization is in part a function of fast-falling transaction costs that reduce the inefficiency of repeated market transactions. With a more efficient market, companies can operate closer to lean start-ups, with increased flexibility to respond to quickly changing market conditions, customer preferences, and technological evolution. In less-efficient markets, specialization is less visible, with inventors continuing to do their own production and designers performing their own assembly.

Two other related trends are driving the evolution and configuration of these ecosystems. One is the creation of best practices to optimize core asset utilization. The second is the development of new tools to better manage the cost of inventory.

Asset utilization increasingly determines the profitability of new products and services. That's because near-perfect market information, as we have seen, helps companies drive demand for their goods and reach new buyers quickly, improving the utilization of fixed assets of production and distribution.

On the flip side, near-perfect market information also means that when a Big Bang Disruptor emerges, all the value can be lost if the innovator can't respond quickly to a sudden spike in demand that in turn drives the acquisition of spare capacity. Given the likelihood of rapid saturation even for successful Big Bang Disruptors, these production assets can, absent a steady stream of new experiments and corresponding market demand, quickly fall to wasteful underutilization.

Idle assets quickly wipe out the profit won from an earlier disruptor. Recall the example of Zynga, which acquired the producer of Draw Something just as the game hit saturation and began its quick descent. Without another hit to replace it, expensive engineering and marketing expertise transformed disastrously from asset to liability.

The second trend driving specialization is improvement in the ability to manage the cost of inventory. Producing too much of even a wildly popular product and failing to recognize imminent market saturation can not only wipe out hard-earned revenue, it can even lead to insolvency. Recall THQ, which ramped up production of its uDraw tablets and developed versions for other gaming platforms just as users were moving on to other devices and applications.

That's the kind of potential disaster that encourages inventors and designers to avoid production altogether, relying instead on producers and assemblers with expertise in lean production and the ability to spread risk over several products and customers. It also drives online sellers such as Amazon and its competitors to use advanced analytics to manage inventories as efficiently as possible.

We introduced twelve rules for success in Big Bang Disruption, and provided dozens of examples of enterprises and entrepreneurs who got it both right and wrong. Many of these stories seemed on first blush counterintuitive. Seen through the lens of exponential technologies and their unique economic properties, however, seemingly random events came into focus as examples of wise decision making—the application of a new model for strategic planning in a world of better and cheaper products and services.

But even the successful launch of a Big Bang Disruptor, in the end, only earns you a license to try again.

As exponential technologies and the disruptors they spawn remake your industry in ever-shorter cycles of creative destruction, the most valuable asset you can have is speed. Pressure from the disruptors relentlessly compresses the life cycle of innovation. Time is of the essence. You have to be quick to spot the failed early market experiments of the Singularity, to survive catastrophic success in the Big Bang, to maximize the residual value of declining assets in the Big Crunch, and to abandon low- or no-profit legacy businesses and customers before you're crushed by the intense gravity of Entropy.

Few companies can operate for long at the pace of exponential change, but then, they don't really have to. One of our favorite old jokes involves two campers who awake to hear a bear rummaging around outside their tent. One of the campers begins to put on his shoes. "What are you doing?" the other asks incredulously. "You can't outrun a bear." "I don't have to," the other one replies. "I just have to outrun you."

How fast do you need to be to outrun the other campers? Here's a good rule of thumb: In our experience, the companies that thrive in Big Bang Disruption are those that have the energy to work at the pace of a start-up, a venture investor, or a young entrepreneur pulling an all-nighter at a hackathon, fueled by unrealistic hopes and too much caffeine.

ACKNOWLEDGMENTS

We have had the help and support of many friends and colleagues in the preparation of this manuscript.

First to be recognized is Ivy Lee, our research lead and all-around make-it-happen person, who never let us experience our own Big Bang Disruption. This book would truly not have happened without her.

We owe special thanks to Julia Kirby, our editor at *Harvard Business Review*, who saw us through many drafts of the March 2013 article that launched this project.

For helpful comments, suggestions, corrections, and insights on the manuscript, our thanks to Eric Apel, Laura Boxer, Carolyn Brandon, Peter Christy, Richard Posner, Hedy Straus, and Adam Thierer. At Accenture, we thank early readers of the manuscript who gave us extraordinarily useful feedback, especially Wayne Borchardt, Dan Elron, Dave Light, David Mann, Mark McDonald, and Sam Yardley.

We are also grateful to many people who were generous with their time in interviews, and in making introductions to people and companies featured in the book. We thank Kevin Ashton, Mark

Chung, Gordon Crovitz, Alex Donn, Deborah Hopkins, David Hornik, Blair Levin, Heidi Mason, Mike Masnick, Laura Mather, James Mawson, Mike McGeary, Chet Pipkin, Jonathan Spalter, and Berin Szoka.

Also at Accenture, we thank those who gave us all manner of feedback, encouragement, and unending support throughout the entire project including Claire Allen, Josh Bellin, Olly Benzecry, Bruno Berthon, Scott Brown, James Collins, Shawn Collinson, Karen Crennan, David Cudaback, Michael Denham, Piercarlo Gera, Trevor Gruzin, Ulf Henning, Nicolai Hesdorf, Hoon-Sang Kim, Dan Huedig, Peter Lacy, Ryan McManus, Narendra Mulani, George Murray, Carlos Niezen, Michael Ostergard, Jean Ostvoll, Younghoon Park, Grant Powell, Olivier Schunck, Sei-Myung Chang, Bob Sell, Baiju Shah, David Y. Smith, Mark Spelman, Roxanne Taylor, John Walsh, Brian Whipple, Robert Wollan, and John Zealley.

Special thanks for true partnership and collegiality go to Bob Thomas, Gwen Harrigan, and all the members and adjuncts of the Accenture Institute for High Performance.

At William Morris Endeavor, our thanks to Eric Lupfer for support above and beyond the duties of a literary agent.

At Penguin Portfolio, our gratitude to Adrian Zackheim and Maria Gagliano.

At *Forbes*, our thanks to Bruce Upbin and Lewis DVorkin.

Last but not least, our profound gratitude for immeasurable help and valuable guidance to Leigh Buchanan; Tim Breene; Anna Caffrey; Shirlee Citron; Dick Costolo; Thomas H. (Tom) Davenport; Aaron Holby; Ajit Kambil; Andrew Keen; Ellen Leander; Andy Lippman; Larry Loo; Sarah Loo; Carl Morison; Kevin Morison; Joan, Jon, Charlotte, and Michael Nunes; Joseph Nunes; Michael Petricone; Gary Shapiro; Rick Stuckey; Hal Varian; and H. James (Jim) Wilson.

BIBLIOGRAPHY

Abelson, Hal, Ken Ledeen, and Harry Lewis, *Blown to Bits: Your Life, Liberty, and Happiness after the Digital Revolution* (Boston: Pearson, 2008)

Bushnell, Nolan and Gene Stone, *Finding the Next Steve Jobs* (Pasadena, CA: Netminds, 2013)

Brynjolfsson, Eric and Andrew McAfee, *Race Against the Machine: How the Digital Revolution is Accelerating Innovation, Driving Productivity, and Irreversibly Transforming Employment and the Economy* (Lexington, KY: Digital Frontier, 2010)

Bygrave, William and Jeffry A. Timmons, *Venture Capital at the Crossroads* (Boston: Harvard Business Review Press, 1992)

Christensen, Clayton M., *The Innovator's Dilemma: When New Technologies Cause Great Firms to Fail* (Boston: Harvard Business Review Press, 1997)

Coase, R. H., *Essays on Economics and Economists* (Chicago: University of Chicago Press, 1995)

Coase, R. H., *The Firm, the Market, and the Law* (Chicago: University of Chicago Press, 1990)

Cowen, Tyler, *The Great Stagnation: How America Ate All the Low-Hanging Fruit of Modern History, Got Sick, and Will (Eventually) Feel Better* (New York: Dutton, 2011)

Downes, Larry, *The Laws of Disruption: Harnessing the New Forces that Govern Life and Business in the Digital Age* (New York: Basic Books, 2009)

Downes, Larry and Chunka Mui, *Unleashing the Killer App: Digital Strategies for Market Dominance* (Boston: Harvard Business Review Press, 1998)

Drucker, Peter, *Concept of the Corporation* (Piscataway, NJ: Transaction, 1993)

Drucker, Peter F., *Post-Capitalist Society* (New York: HarperBusiness, 1993)

Freeman, Chris and Francisco Louçã, *As Time Goes By: From the Industrial Revolutions to the Information Revolution* (Oxford: Oxford University Press, 2001)

Hagel, John III, John Seely Brown, and Lang Davidson, *The Power of Pull: How Small Moves, Smartly Made, Can Set Big Things in Motion* (New York: Basic Books, 2010)

Hamel, Gary and C. K. Prahalad, *Competing for the Future* (Boston: Harvard Business Review Press, 1996)

Kim, W. Chan and Renée Mauborgne, *Blue Ocean Strategy: How to Create Uncontested Market Space and Make Competition Irrelevant* (Boston: Harvard Business Review Press, 2005)

Kuhn, Thomas S., *The Structure of Scientific Revolutions* (Chicago: University of Chicago Press, 1962)

Levitt, Steven D. and Stephen J. Dubner, *Freakonomics: A Rogue Economist Explores the Hidden Side of Everything* (New York: Harper Perennial, 2009)

Mason, Heidi and Tim Rohner, *The Venture Imperative: A New Model for Corporate Innovation* (Boston: Harvard Business Review Press, 2002)

McGahan, Anita M., *How Industries Evolve: Principles for Achieving and Sustaining Superior Performance* (Boston: Harvard Business Review Press, 2004)

McGraw, Thomas K., *Prophet of Innovation: Joseph Schumpeter and Creative Destruction* (Boston: Harvard University Press, 2010)

Mintzberg, Henry, *Rise and Fall of Strategic Planning* (New York: Free Press, 1994)

Moore, Geoffrey A., *Crossing the Chasm: Marketing and Selling Disruptive Products to Mainstream Customers* (New York: HarperCollins, 1991)

Moore, Geoffrey A., *Inside the Tornado: Marketing Strategies from Silicon Valley's Cutting Edge* (New York: HarperBusiness, 1995)

Nairn, Alasdair, *Engines that Move Markets: Technology Investing from Railroads to the Internet and Beyond* (New York: Wiley, 2002)

Negroponte, Nicholas, *Being Digital* (New York: Vintage, 1996)

Nunes, Paul and Tim Breene, *Jumping the S-Curve: How to Beat the Growth Cycle, Get on Top, and Stay There* (Boston: Harvard Business Review Press, 2011)

Perez, Carlota, *Technological Revolutions and Financial Capital: The Dynamics of Bubbles and Golden Ages* (Cheltenham: Edgar Elgar Publishing, 2002)

Porter, Michael E., *Competitive Advantage: Creating and Sustaining Superior Performance* (New York: Free Press, 1985)

Postrel, Virginia, *The Future and Its Enemies* (New York: Free Press, 1999)

Schmidt, Eric and Jared Cohen, *The New Digital Age: Reshaping the Future of People, Nations, and Businesses* (New York: Knopf, 2013)

Schumpeter, Joseph A., *Capitalism, Socialism and Democracy 3d. Ed.* (New York: Harper & Brothers, 1950)

Shapiro, Carl and Hal R. Varian, *Information Rules: A Strategic Guide to the Network Economy* (Boston: Harvard Business Review Press, 1998)

Stigler, George J., *The Organization of Industry* (Chicago: University of Chicago Press, 1983)

Treacy, Michael and Fred Wiersema, *The Discipline of Market Leaders: Choose Your Customers, Narrow Your Focus, Dominate Your Market* (New York: Basic Books, 1997)

INDEX

Page numbers in *italics* refer to illustrations.

ERIC RIES

THE LEAN STARTUP: How Constant Innovation Creates Radically Successful Businesses

Most new businesses fail. But most of those failures are preventable.

The Lean Startup is a new approach to business that's being adopted around the world. It is changing the way companies are built and new products are launched.

The Lean Startup is about learning what your customers really want. It's about testing your vision continuously, adapting and adjusting before it's too late.

Now is the time to think Lean.

'Every so often a business book comes along that changes how we think about innovation and entrepreneurship. Eric Ries's *The Lean Startup* has the chops to join this exalted company.' Philip Delves Broughton, *Financial Times*

'Mandatory reading for entrepreneurs... loaded with fascinating stories and practical principles' Dan Heath, co-author of *Switch* and *Made to Stick*

'If you are an entrepreneur, read this book. If you are thinking about becoming an entrepreneur, read this book. If you are just curious about entrepreneurship, read this book.' Randy Komisar, Founding Director of TiVo

'*The Lean Startup* will change the way we think about entrepreneurship' Tom Eisenmann, Professor of Entrepreneurship, Harvard Business School

START WITH WHY
BY SIMON SINEK

The TED Talks sensation and global bestseller

Why are some people and organizations more inventive, pioneering and successful than others? And why are they able to repeat their success again and again?

Because in business it doesn't matter what you do, it matters why you do it.

Steve Jobs, the Wright brothers and Martin Luther King have one thing in common: they STARTED WITH WHY.

This book is for anyone who wants to inspire others, or to be inspired.

www.startwithwhy.com

KHOI TU

SUPERTEAMS: The Secrets of Stellar Performance

What do the SAS, Ferrari and the Rolling Stones have in common? Their success is about much more than talented individuals. They are Superteams.

Every organisation, whether a business or a sports club, lives or dies by the quality of its teamwork. No man can be an island for long; only great teams can face a crisis and emerge stronger.

So how do you build the right team? Many people think of it like a rock supergroup: bring the best of the best together and magic will happen. Yet supergroups often flop, while bands of unknowns rise to the top.

In this incisive and inspirational book, renowned teamwork specialist Khoi Tu explains how to make sure your team delivers consistently superior results, whatever your aim: averting business failure or resolving political conflict, dealing with a hostage situation or leading your team to sporting victory.

Superteams takes ten legendary teams - including animation studio Pixar, Europe's 2010 Rider Cup winners, and the people behind the Northern Ireland peace process - and analyses their inner workings, evolution and defining moments. The route to excellence, Khoi Tu argues, lies in the seven tasks that will turn your team into a superteam: a compelling trigger (crusade or crisis); seriously talented but adaptable team members; meticulous preparation; perfectly balanced structure; powerful team culture; first-class leadership development; and a blend of *per ardua ad astra* and *Who Dares Wins*.

'Khoi Tu is the most visionary among visionaries' John Lloyd, *Management Today*